Writing for Social Scientists

Chicago Guides
to *Writing*, Editing,
and Publishing

Writing for Social Scientists

How to Start and
Finish Your Thesis,
Book, or Article

Howard S. Becker
with a chapter by
Pamela Richards

The University of Chicago Press
Chicago and London

The drawings reproduced at the chapter openings of this book are by
Claire Bretécher and first appeared under the title "Création" in *Les
Frustrés 3*, © Le Nouvel Observateur.

Chapter 1 appeared, in slightly different form, in *The Sociological
Quarterly*, vol. 24 (Autumn 1983), and is reprinted here with the
permission of the Midwest Sociological Society.

The University of Chicago Press, Chicago 60637
The University of Chicago Press, Ltd., London
© 1986 by The University of Chicago
All rights reserved. Published 1986
Printed in the United States of America

95 94 93 92 91 90 89 88 87   543

Library of Congress Cataloging-in-Publication Data

Becker, Howard Saul, 1928–
  Writing for social scientists.

  Bibliography; p.
  Includes index.
  1. Social sciences—Authorship.   2. Sociology—
Authorship.   I. Title.
H91.B4 1986   808'.0663   85-16504
ISBN 0-226-04107-7 (cloth)
      0-226-04108-5 (paper)

Contents

Preface

Several years ago I began to teach a seminar in writing for graduate students in sociology at Northwestern University. As the first chapter explains, I found myself giving private lessons and therapy to so many people that it seemed economical to deal with them all at once. The experience was so interesting, and the need for something like that class so obvious, that I wrote a paper (the present first chapter) describing it. I sent the paper to a few people, mostly students who had taken the class and some friends. They, and others who eventually read it, suggested other topics that could profitably be covered, so I kept on writing.

I had expected that helpful response from friends and colleagues, especially those in sociology, but not the mail that began to arrive, from all over the country, from people I didn't know, who had gotten the paper from a friend and found it useful. Some of the letters were very emotional. The authors said that they had

been having great trouble writing and that just reading the paper had given them the confidence to try again. Sometimes they wondered how someone who didn't know them could describe their fears and worries in such precise detail. I liked the paper but knew it wasn't that good. In fact, most of the specific advice in it was commonplace in English composition classes and books. I supposed that my readers found the paper so pertinent and useful because, in a version of C. Wright Mills's distinction between "the personal troubles of milieu" and "the public issues of social structure" (1959, 8–11), it did not analyze unique private problems at all, but common difficulties built into academic life. The paper dealt only with problems of sociological writing (I am, after all, a sociologist by trade), but the letters, surprisingly, came from people in fields as diverse as art history and computer science.

Although what I had to say seemed useful to this variety of people, I don't know enough about all those fields to talk knowledgeably about their specific difficulties. I have focused, therefore, on the specific problems of writing about society, especially in sociology, and leave readers from other fields to make the translations for themselves. That translation should be easy because so many sociological classics now belong to the intellectual world at large. Durkheim, Weber, and Marx speak to a larger audience than the American Sociological Association.

A large number of excellent books on writing already exists (for instance, Strunk and White 1959; Gowers 1954; Zinsser 1980; and Williams 1981). I read some of them in the course of teaching my class but did not know then that there was a field of research and speculation called "composition theory." As a result, I invented ideas and procedures already invented by others and discussed in that field's literature. I have since tried to repair my ignorance and refer readers throughout to these lengthier descriptions. Many books on composition contain excellent advice on the com-

mon faults of writing, especially academic writing.
They warn against passive constructions, wordiness,
using long foreign-sounding words where small American ones would do better, and other common errors.
They give solid, specific advice on how to find your
mistakes and deal with them. Other writers (for example, Shaughnessy 1977; Elbow 1981; or Schultz 1982)
talk about these problems too—it's impossible to talk
about writing without mentioning them—but go further
and analyze why writing itself is such a problem. They
tell how to overcome the paralyzing fear of having
others read your work. Their years of experience teaching writing to undergraduates shows in the specificity
of their advice and in their greater attention to the
process of writing than to results. The best research on
writing (see, for instance, Flower 1979 and Flower and
Hayes 1981) analyzes the *process* of writing and con-
cludes that writing is a form of thinking. If that's true,
the advice often given to writers—first get your thought
clear, and only then try to state it clearly—is wrong.
Their results give some support to my own practice and
teaching.

Standard texts in composition traditionally address
college undergraduates (not surprisingly, since that is
where the market and the need are strongest), though
they generally say, correctly, that people in business,
government and the academy might profit from them
too. But the graduate students and scholars I work with
(in sociology and other fields) have all had Freshman
English, very likely taught by people who know the
modern theories of composition and use the new methods, and it hasn't helped them. They have been told to
use active constructions and short words, to make sure
their pronouns and antecedents agree, and similar
useful things, but they don't follow the advice. They
don't consult the composition books that might help
them write clearer prose, and probably would ignore
their useful advice if they did. They even ignore the
scoldings their own colleagues periodically offer (see,

for instance, Selvin and Wilson 1984 and Merton's parody, "Foreword to a Preface for an Introduction to a Prolegomenon to a Discourse on a Certain Subject" [1969]). A book meant to help them must deal with *why* they write that way, given that they know they shouldn't. It must not only show them what they've done wrong and how to fix it, but also move from the situation of the undergraduate to their very different one.

Undergraduates don't have the same problems with writing that older people have. They write short essays they would not write of their own choice, in a few weeks, on subjects they know nothing about and aren't interested in, for a reader who, as Shaughnessy says, "would not choose to read it if he were not being paid to be an examiner" (1977, 86). They know that what they write in this one paper will not affect their lives much. Sociologists and other scholars, on the other hand, write about subjects they know a lot about and care about even more. They write for people they hope are equally interested, and they have no deadlines, other than those their professional situations impose on them. They know that their professional futures rest on how peers and superiors judge what they write. Students can distance themselves from their required writing. Scholars, novice or professional, can't. They impose the task on themselves by entering their discipline and have to take it seriously. Being serious, writing scares them more than it does students (Pamela Richards describes the fear in Chapter 6, below), which makes the technical problems even harder to solve.

I have not, despite the title of the opening chapter, rewritten a freshman English text for use by graduate students. I can't compete with the classic works in English composition, whose authors know more about grammar, syntax and the other classic topics than I do or ever will, and I haven't tried. Some of these matters appear briefly, largely because I am pretty sure that graduate students and young professionals in sociology

and related disciplines simply will not search out or pay attention to advice from outside their own field. They ought to. But if writing about society will improve only when sociologists study grammar and syntax seriously, it never will. Further, problems of style and diction invariably involve matters of substance. Bad sociological writing, as I argue later, can't be separated from the theoretical problems of the discipline. Finally, the way people write grows out of the social situations they write in. So we need to see (this summarizes the book's perspective) how social organization creates the classic problems of scholarly writing: style, organization, and the rest. Instead of trying to write a Freshman English book I'm not competent to write, then, I have tried to meet the need for an analysis that addresses the peculiar problems of writing about society by approaching the technical problems other authors write about sociologically. I deal specifically with scholarly, and especially sociological, writing and set its problems in the context of scholarly work. (Most of Sternberg's "How to Complete and Survive a Doctoral Dissertation" is concerned with the politics of the process—choosing dissertation advisers, for instance—rather than with the actual writing.)

I have, immodestly, written personally and autobiographically. Others have done that (Peter Elbow, for one), probably for the same reason I did. Students find it hard to imagine writing as a real activity that real people do. As Shaughnessy (1977, 79) says, "The beginning writer does not know how writers behave." Students do not think of books as the result of someone's work. Even graduate students, who are much closer to their instructors, seldom see anyone actually writing, seldom see working drafts and writing that isn't ready for publication. It's a mystery to them: I want to remove the mystery and let them see that the work they read is made by people who have the same difficulties they do. My prose is not exemplary, but since I know what went into its making, I can discuss

why I wrote it that way, what the problems were and how I chose solutions. I can't do that with anyone else's work. Since I have been producing sociological writing for over thirty years, many students and young professionals have read some of it, and readers of this book in manuscript have said that it is useful to know that those pieces troubled and confused me in the same way their work bothers them. For that reason, I have devoted a chapter to my own experiences as a writer.

Chapter 1 originally appeared, in a slightly different form, in The Sociological Quarterly, 24 (Autumn 1983): 575–88, and is reprinted here with the permission of the Midwest Sociological Society.

I thank all the people who helped me, especially (in addition to the people in the classes I have taught) Kathryn Pyne Addelson, James Bennett, James Clark, Dan Dixon, Blanche Geer, Robert A. Gundlach, Christopher Jencks, Michael Joyce, Sheila Levine, Leo Litwak, Michal McCall, Donald McCloskey, Robert K. Merton, Harvey Molotch, Arline Meyer, Michael Schudson, Gilberto Velho, John Walton, and Joseph M.Williams. I am especially grateful to Rosanna Hertz for writing the letter that prompted the chapter "Persona and Authority" and for letting me quote from it so extensively. A letter Pamela Richards wrote to me about risk was so complete as it stood that I asked her if she would let it appear in this volume under her name. I'm glad she agreed. I couldn't have said it half so well.

One

Freshman English for Graduate Students

A Memoir and Two Theories

I have taught a seminar on writing for graduate students several times. This requires a certain amount of "chutzpah." After all, to teach a topic suggests that you know something about it. Writing professionally, as a sociologist, for almost thirty years, gave me some claim to that knowledge. In addition, several teachers and colleagues had not only criticized my prose, but had given me innumerable lessons meant to improve it. On the other hand, everyone knows that sociologists write very badly, so that literary types can make jokes about bad writing just by saying "sociology," the way vaudeville comedians used to get a laugh just by saying "Peoria" or "Cucamonga." (See, for instance, Cowley's [1956] attack and Merton's [1972] reply.) The experience and lessons haven't saved me from the faults I still share with my colleagues.

Nevertheless, I took the chance, driven to it by stories of the chronic problems students and fellow

sociologists had with writing. I listed the course.

The turnout for the first class surprised me. Not only did ten or twelve graduate students sign up, the class also contained a couple of post-Ph.D. researchers and even a few of my younger faculty colleagues, and that pattern of enrollment continued in succeeding years. Their worries and troubles with writing overshadowed the fear of embarrassing themselves by going back to school.

My "chutzpah" went beyond teaching a course whose subject I was no master of. I didn't even prepare for the class, because (being a sociologist, not a teacher of composition) I had no idea how to teach it. So I walked in the first day not knowing what I would do. After a few fumbling preliminary remarks, I had a flash. I had been reading the *Paris Review Interviews with Writers* for years and had always had a slightly prurient interest in what the interviewed authors shamelessly revealed about their writing habits. So I turned to a former graduate student and old friend sitting on my left and said, "Louise, how do you write?" I explained that I was not interested in any fancy talk about scholarly preparations but, rather, in the nitty-gritty details, whether she typed or wrote in longhand, used any special kind of paper or worked at any special time of day. I didn't know what she would say.

The hunch paid off. She gave, more or less unself-consciously, a lengthy account of an elaborate routine which had to be done just so. Although she was not embarrassed by what she described, others squirmed a little as she explained that she could only write on yellow, ruled, legal-size pads using a green felt-tip pen, that she had to clean the house first (that turned out to be a common preliminary for women but not for men, who were more likely to sharpen twenty pencils), that she could only write between such and such hours, and so on.

I knew I was on to something and went on to the next victim. A little more reluctantly, he described his

equally peculiar habits. The third one said he was sorry but he'd like to pass his turn. I didn't allow that. He had a good reason, as it turned out. They all did. By then they could see that what people were describing was something quite shameful, nothing you wanted to talk about in front of twenty other people. I was relentless, making everyone tell all and not sparing myself.

This exercise created great tension, but also a lot of joking, enormous interest, and eventually a surprising relaxation. I pointed out that they all were relieved, and ought to be, because, while their worst fears were true—they really were crazy—they were no crazier than anyone else. It was a common disease. Just as people feel relieved to discover that some frightening physical symptoms they've been hiding are just something that is "going around," knowing that others had crazy writing habits should have been, and clearly was, a good thing.

I went on with my interpretation. From one point of view, my fellow participants were describing neurotic symptoms. Viewed sociologically, however, those symptoms were magical rituals. According to Malinowski (1948, 25–36), people perform such rituals to influence the result of some process over which they think they have no rational means of control. He described the phenomenon as he observed it among the Trobriand Islanders:

> Thus in canoe building empirical knowledge of material, of technology, and of certain principles of stability and hydrodynamics, function in company and in close association with magic, each yet uncontaminated by the other.
> For example, they understand perfectly well that the wider the span of the outrigger the greater the stability yet the smaller the resistance against strain. They can clearly explain why they have to give this span a certain traditional width, measured in fractions of the length of the dugout.

They can also explain, in rudimentary but clearly mechanical terms, how they have to behave in a sudden gale, why the outrigger must always be on the weather side, why the one type of canoe can and the other cannot beat. They have, in fact, a whole system of principles of sailing, embodied in a complex and rich terminology, traditionally handed on and obeyed as rationally and consistently as is modern science by modern sailors. . . .

But even with all their systematic knowledge, methodically applied, they are still at the mercy of powerful and incalculable tides, sudden gales during the monsoon season and unknown reefs. And here comes in their magic, performed over the canoe during its construction, carried out at the beginning and in the course of expeditions and resorted to in moments of real danger. (30–31)

Just like the Trobriand sailors, sociologists who couldn't handle the dangers of writing in a rational way used magical charms, that dispelled anxiety, though without really affecting the result.

So I asked the class: What are you so afraid of not being able to control rationally that you have to use all these magical spells and rituals? I'm no Freudian, but I did think they would resist answering the question. They didn't. On the contrary, they spoke easily and at length. They feared, to summarize the long discussion that followed, two things. They were afraid that they would not be able to organize their thoughts, that writing would be a big, confusing chaos that would drive them mad. They spoke feelingly about a second fear, that what they wrote would be "wrong" and that (unspecified) people would laugh at them. That seemed to account for more of the ritual. A second person who wrote on legal-sized, yellow, ruled tablets always started on the second page. Why? Well, she said, if anyone walked by, you could pull down the top sheet and cover what you had been writing so the passerby couldn't see.

Many of the rituals ensured that what was written could not be taken for a "finished" product, so no one could laugh at it. The excuse was built in. I think that's why even writers who type well often use such time-wasting methods as longhand. Anything written in longhand is clearly not yet done and so cannot be criticized as though it were. You can keep people from taking your writing as a serious expression of your abilities even more surely, however, by not writing at all. No one can read what has never been put on paper.

Something important had happened in that class. As I also pointed out to them that first day, they had all told something quite shameful about themselves, and no one had died. (Here what had happened resembled what might be called the "new California therapies," which rely on people revealing their psyches or bodies in public and discovering that the revelation, similarly, does not kill.) It surprised me that people in this class, many of whom knew each other quite well, knew nothing at all about each other's work habits and, in fact, had hardly ever seen each other's writing. I decided to do something about that.

I had originally told prospective class members that the class would emphasize, instead of writing, copy editing and rewriting. Therefore I made the price of admission to the class an already written paper on which they would now practice rewriting. Before tackling these papers, however, I decided to show them what it meant to rewrite and edit. A colleague lent me a rough second draft of a paper she was working on. I distributed her three or four page "methods section" at the beginning of the second class, and we spent three hours rewriting it.

Sociologists habitually use twenty words where two will do, and we spent most of that afternoon cutting excess words. I used a trick I had often used in private lessons. With my pencil poised over a word or clause, I asked, "Does this need to be here? If not, I'm taking it out." I insisted that we must not, in making any change,

lose the slightest nuance of the author's thought. (I had in mind here the rules C. Wright Mills followed in his well-known "translation" of passages from Talcott Parsons [Mills 1959, 27–31].) If no one defended the word or phrase, I took it out. I changed passive to active constructions, combined sentences, took long sentences apart—all the things these students had once learned to do in freshman composition. At the end of three hours, we had reduced four pages to three-quarters of a page without losing any nuance or essential detail.

We worked on one long sentence—which considered the possible implications of what the paper had so far said—for quite a while, removing words and phrases until it was a quarter as long as it had been. I finally suggested (mischievously, but they weren't sure of that) that we cut the whole thing and just say, "So what?" Someone finally broke the stunned silence: "You could get away with that, but we couldn't." So we talked about tone, concluding that I couldn't get away with it either, unless I had properly prepared for that sort of tone, and it was appropriate to the occasion.

The students felt very sorry for my colleague who had donated the pages we did this surgery on. They thought she had been humiliated, that it was lucky she hadn't been there to die of shame. In empathizing like that, they relied on their own unprofessional feelings, not realizing that people who write professionally, and write a lot, routinely rewrite as we just had. I wanted them to believe that this was not unusual and that they should expect to rewrite a lot, so I told them (truthfully) that I habitually rewrote manuscripts eight to ten times before publication (although not before giving them to my friends to read). Since, as I'll explain later, they thought that "good writers" (people like their teachers) got everything right the first time, that shocked them.

This exercise had several results. The students were exhausted, never having spent so much time on or looked so closely at one piece of writing, never having

imagined that anyone *could* spend so much time on such a job. They had seen and experimented with a number of standard editorial devices. But the most important result came at the end of the afternoon when, exhaustedly, one student—that wonderful student who says what others are thinking but know better than to say—said, "Gee, Howie, when you say it this way, it looks like something anybody could say." You bet.

We talked about that. Was it what you said that was sociological, or was it the way you said it? Mind you, we had not replaced any technical sociological language. That had not been the problem (it almost never is). We had replaced redundancies, "fancy writing," pompous phrases (for instance, my personal bête noire, "the way in which," for which a plain "how" can usually be substituted without losing anything but pretentiousness)—anything that could be simplified without damage to the thought. We decided that authors tried to give substance and weight to what they wrote by sounding academic, even at the expense of their real meaning.

We discovered some other things that interminable afternoon. Some of those long, redundant expressions couldn't be replaced because they had no underlying sense to replace. They were placeholders, marking a spot where the author should have said something plainer but had at the moment nothing plain to say. These spots nevertheless had to be filled because otherwise the author would only have half a sentence. Writers did not use these meaningless phrases and sentences randomly or simply because they had bad writing habits. Certain situations evoked meaningless placeholders.

Writers routinely use meaningless expressions to cover up two kinds of problems. Both kinds of problems reflect serious dilemmas of sociological theory. One problem has to do with agency: who did the things that your sentence alleges were done? Sociologists often prefer locutions that leave the answer to that

question unclear, largely because many of their theories don't tell them who is doing what. In many sociological theories, things just happen without anyone doing them. It's hard to find a subject for a sentence when "larger social forces" or "inexorable social processes" are at work. Avoiding saying who did it produces two characteristic faults of sociological writing: the habitual use of passive constructions and abstract nouns.

If you say, for example, that "deviants were labeled," you don't have to say who labeled them. That is a theoretical error, not just bad writing. A major point of the labeling theory of deviance (outlined in Becker 1963) is precisely that someone labels the person deviant, someone with the power to do it and good reasons for wanting to. If you leave those actors out, you misstate the theory, both in letter and spirit. Yet it is a common locution. Sociologists commit similar theoretical errors when they say that society does this or that or that culture makes people do things, and sociologists do write that way all the time.

Sociologists' inability or unwillingness to make causal statements similarly leads to bad writing. David Hume's *Essay Concerning Human Understanding* made us all nervous about claiming to demonstrate causal connections, and though few sociologists are as skeptical as Hume, most understand that despite the efforts of John Stuart Mill, the Vienna Circle and all the rest, they run serious scholarly risks when they allege that A causes B. Sociologists have many ways of describing how elements covary, most of them vacuous expressions hinting at what we would like, but don't dare, to say. Since we are afraid to say that A causes B, we say, "There is a tendency for them to covary" or "They seem to be associated."

The reasons for doing this bring us back to the rituals of writing. We write that way because we fear that others will catch us in obvious errors if we do anything else, and laugh at us. Better to say something innocuous

but safe than something bold you might not be able to defend against criticism. Mind you, it would not be objectionable to say, "A varies with B," if that was what you really wanted to say, and it is certainly reasonable to say, "I think A causes B and my data support that by showing that they covary." But many people use such expressions to hint at stronger assertions they just don't want to take the rap for. They want to discover causes, because causes are scientifically interesting, but don't want the philosophical responsibility.

Every teacher of English composition and every guide to writing criticizes passive constructions, abstract nouns, and most of the other faults I mentioned. I did not invent these standards. In fact, I learned them in composition classes myself. Although the standards are thus independent of any particular school of thought, I believe that my preference for clarity and directness also has roots in the symbolic interactionist tradition of sociology, which focuses on real actors in real situations. My Brazilian colleague Gilberto Velho insists that these are ethnocentric standards, strongly favored in the Anglo-American tradition of plain speaking, but having no more warrant than the more flowery, indirect style of some European traditions. I think that's wrong, since some of the best writers in other languages also use a direct style.

Similarly, Michael Schudson asked me, not unreasonably, how someone ought to write who believes that structures—capitalist relations of production, for instance—cause social phenomena. Should such a theorist use passive constructions to indicate the passivity of the human actors involved? That question requires two answers. The simpler is that few serious theories of society leave no room for human agency. More importantly, passive constructions even hide the agency attributed to systems and structures. Suppose a system does the labeling of deviants. Saying "deviants are labeled" covers that up too.

Much of what we removed from my colleague's paper in class consisted of what I named, for class purposes (with Wayne Booth's criticism of academic "Greek-fed, polysyllabic bullshit" (Booth 1979, 277) as legitimating precedent), "bullshit qualifications," vague phrases expressing a general readiness to abandon the point being made if anyone objects: "A tends to be related to B," "A might possibly tend to be related to B under some conditions," and similar cowardly qualifiers. A real qualification says that A is related to B except under certain specified circumstances: I always shop for groceries at the Safeway unless it's closed; the positive relationship between income and education is stronger if you are white than if you are black. But the students, like other sociologists, habitually used less specific qualifications. They wanted to say that the relationship existed, but knew that someone would, sooner or later, find an exception. The nonspecific, ritual qualifier gave them an all-purpose loophole. If attacked, they could say they never said it was always true. Bullshit qualifications, making your statements fuzzy, ignore the philosophical and methodological tradition which holds that making generalizations in a strong universal form identifies negative evidence which can be used to improve them.

As I asked people in the class about why they wrote the way they did, I learned that they had picked up many of their habits in high school and solidified them in college. What they had learned to write were term papers (see Shaughnessy's [1977, 85–6] discussion of the conditions of undergraduate writing). You write a term paper by doing whatever reading or research is required throughout the term and working out the paper in your head as you go along. But you write only one draft, perhaps after making an outline, usually the night before handing it in. Like a Japanese brush painting, you do it, and either it's OK or it isn't. College students have no time for rewriting, since they often have several papers due at the same time. The method

works for undergraduates. Some become very adept at the format and turn out creditable, highly polished papers, working on them in their heads as they walk around campus, putting the words on paper as the assignments come due. Teachers know all this. If they aren't aware of the mechanics, they know the typical results and don't expect papers more coherent or highly polished than such a method can produce.

Students who habitually work that way understandably worry about the draft they produce. They know it could be better but is not going to be. Whatever they put down is *it*. As long as that document is kept confidential, in the conventionally private teacher-undergraduate relationship, it won't embarass the author too much.

But the social organization of writing and reputation changes in graduate school. Teachers talk about your papers, for good or bad, to their colleagues and to other students. With luck, the papers grow into qualifying papers or dissertations, read by several faculty members.

Graduate students also write longer papers than undergraduates do. Students expert at the one-shot term paper cannot hold a longer paper in their heads so easily. That's when they start losing their ability to write. They cannot produce a one-draft paper and be confident that it will not provoke ridicule and criticism. So they don't write.

I didn't tell the students all this during the first class sessions, though I eventually did. Instead, I gave assignments that would get them to give up the one-draft method of producing papers. They might then find alternate routines that were less painful and equally effective in earning academic rewards. A few adventurous students in each of the several classes I have taught have trusted me enough to go along with these experiments. My reputation for not being fierce weakened the traditional student fear of professors, and those who had taken other classes with me trusted my eccentricities. Teachers who lack that advantage might have more trouble using some of these tricks.

I told students that it didn't make much difference what they wrote in a first draft because they could always change it. Since what they put on a piece of paper was not necessarily final, they needn't worry so much about what they wrote. The only version that mattered was the last one. They had gotten a hint of how things could be changed and I promised to show them more.

Our classroom editing and my interpretation of it sobered the students. I asked them to bring the papers I had required as a prerequisite for admission to the class (but had not yet collected) to the next session. (Some students balked at this. The second year I taught the course, one said she wasn't going to bring a paper because she didn't have one. I got angry: "Anyone who has been going to school as long as you have has plenty of papers. Bring one." Then the real reason came out: "I don't have one that's good enough.") After collecting the papers and shuffling them thoroughly, I passed them out again, making sure that no one got his or her own. I asked them to edit the papers thoroughly. The next week they returned them to their authors. Students sat soberly, looking to see what had been done. Plenty, was the answer. There was red ink everywhere.

I asked them how they liked editing someone else's paper. They spoke at length, angrily. They had been surprised by how much work there was to do, at how many silly mistakes people made. After an hour of complaining, I asked them how they liked having their papers edited. Again they spoke angrily, but this time they complained that the person who read their paper lacked compassion, couldn't see what they had meant, had changed their text to say things they hadn't intended at all. The smarter ones soon realized that they were talking about themselves, and the group fell silent as that sank in. I said it was a lesson they ought to think about, and that now they could see that they had to write so that well-meaning editors—and they had to assume their colleagues were well-meaning—could not mistake their meaning. Editors and colleagues would often rewrite their work, I told them, and they had better get used to it and not let their feelings be hurt by such experiences. They should try instead to write so clearly that no one could misunderstand and make changes they didn't like.

Then I said that they could really start by writing almost anything, any kind of a rough draft, no matter how crude or confused, and make something good out of it. To prove it, I had to get someone to produce a first, uncensored draft, some ideas written with little care and no corrections. I explained that such a draft would help them find out what they might have to say. (This was one of the places where I invented what I did not know was likewise being developed by people in composition theory. Linda Flower [1979, 36], for instance, describes and analyzes the same procedure as "Writer-Based prose," which "allows the writer freedom to generate a breadth of information and a variety of alternative relationships before locking himself or herself into a premature formulation.") It took some work to find someone who would try such a risky process. I distributed copies of the resulting document to the class.

The person who contributed the piece made some nervous self-deprecating jokes about putting herself in jeopardy by allowing people to see it. To her surprise, what she had written amazed her classmates. They could see that it was mixed-up and written badly, but they could also see, and said, that she had some really interesting ideas there that could be developed. They also openly admired her courage. (Other brave students have had the same effect on their peers in succeeding years.)

This draft showed the author approaching her subject circuitously (like the writers described in Flower and Hayes 1981), not sure of what she wanted to say, saying the same thing in several different ways. Comparing the versions made it easy to see the idea she had been circling around and to formulate it more concisely. We found three or four ideas to work with in that way and could see, or sense, some connections between them. We agreed that the way to work with such a draft was to take notes on it, see what it contained, and then make an outline for another draft. Why bother avoiding redundancy or any of the other faults we had worked so hard to eliminate the week before, since it would be easy to get rid of them, using those newly learned skills, later? Worrying about those faults might slow you down, keep you from saying something in one of the ways that would give you the clue you needed. Better to edit afterward, rather than as you went. The students began to see that writing need not be a one-shot, all-or-nothing venture. It could have stages, each with its own criteria of excellence (as Flower and others could have told them, but perhaps it was better for them to discover it in their own experience). An insistence on clarity and polish appropriate to a late version was entirely inapproppriate to earlier ones meant to get the ideas on paper. In coming to these conclusions, they replicated some of Flower's results and began to understand that worrying about rules of writing too early in the process could keep them from saying what they actually had to say (a point made in the language of cognitive psychology in Rose 1983).

I don't want to exaggerate. My students did not throw away their crutches and start to dance. But they saw that there were ways out of their troubles, which was all I had hoped for. Knowing what was possible, they could try it. Just knowing wasn't enough, of course. They had to use these devices, make them part of their writing routine, perhaps replacing some of the magical elements we had discussed.

We did a number of other things in the seminar. We discussed rhetoric, reading Gusfield (1981) on the rhetoric of social science, and Orwell's "Politics and the

English Language" (1954). Surprisingly, Gusfield the sociologist had a stronger impact than Orwell the writer. He showed how writers in the students' own field manipulated stylistic devices to sound "scientific," particularly noting how passive constructions could produce a facade of impersonality the investigator could hide behind. We talked about scientific writing as a form of rhetoric, meant to persuade, and which forms of persuasion the scientific community considered okay and which illegitimate. I insisted on the rhetorical nature of scientific writing, although the students believed, with many of their elders, that some ways of writing illegitimately attempt to persuade while others just presented the facts and let them speak for themselves. (Sociologists of science and students of rhetoric have written extensively on this point. See, especially, Bazerman 1981, and Latour and Bastide 1983 and the accompanying bibliography.)

That student I was so fond of helped me out again here. After we had discussed the rhetoric of science at length, he said, "Okay, Howie, I know you never like to tell us what to do, but are you going to tell us or not?" "Tell you what?" "How to write without using rhetoric!" As before, everyone had been hoping that I would reveal that secret. Just hearing it said aloud confirmed their worst fears. They couldn't write without using rhetoric and therefore they couldn't evade questions of style.

During several years of teaching the course, I developed a theory of writing which describes the process that produces both the writing people do and the difficulties they have doing it. (The theory, in a more general form, appears in *Art Worlds* [Becker 1982a], as a theory of the making of art works of all kinds. Though it grows out of a sociological social psychology quite different from the cognitive psychology dominating work in composition theory, my notions resemble those of Flower and Hayes and their colleagues.) Any work's eventual form results from all the choices made by all the people involved in producing it. When we write, we constantly make such choices as which idea to take up when; what words to use, in what order, to express it, what examples to give to make our meaning clearer. Of course, writing actually follows an even lengthier process of absorbing and developing ideas, similarly preceded by a process of absorbing impressions and sorting them out. Each choice shapes the result.

If that is a reasonable analysis, we kid ourselves when we think, sitting down to write, that we are composing freshly and can write anything at all. Our earlier choices—to look at it this way, to think about this example in developing our ideas, to use this way of gathering and storing data, to read this novel or watch that television program—rule out what we might otherwise have chosen. Every time we answer a question about our work and what we have been finding or thinking, our choice of words affects the way we describe it the next time, perhaps when we are writing notes or making outlines.

Most of the students had a more conventional view, embodied in the folk maxim that if you think clearly, you will write clearly. They thought they had to work everything out before they wrote Word One, having first assembled all their impressions, ideas, and data and explicitly decided every important question of theory and fact. Otherwise, they might get it wrong. They acted the belief out ritually by not beginning to write until they had every book and note they might possibly need piled up on their desks. They further thought they had a free choice in most of these matters, which led to remarks like "I think I'll use Durkheim for my theory section," as if they hadn't already decided the theoretical issues that invoking Durkheim (or Weber or Marx) had suggested long before, in the way they had done their work. (Scholars in other fields will know which Great Names to substitute here.)

My theory leads to the opposite view: you have already made many choices when you sit down to write, but probably don't know what they were. That leads, naturally, to some confusion, to a mixed-up early draft. But a mixed-up draft is no cause for shame. Rather, it shows you what your earlier choices were, what ideas, theoretical viewpoints, and conclusions you had already committed yourself to before you began writing. Knowing that you will write many more drafts, you know that you need not worry about this one's crudeness and lack of coherence. This one is for discovery, not for presentation (the distinction is C. Wright Mills's [1959, 222], following Reichenbach).

Writing an early rough draft, then, shows you all the earlier decisions that now shape what you can write. You cannot "use" Marx if Durkheim's ideas shaped your thinking. You cannot write about what the data you gathered don't tell you about, or your method of storing them doesn't let you use them for. You see what you have and don't have, what you have already done and already know, and what is left to do. You see that the only job left—even though you have just begun to write—is to make it all clearer. The rough draft shows you what needs to be made clearer; the skills of rewriting and copy editing let you do it.

It's not that easy, of course. The next choices, made in editing and rewriting, also shape the result. You can no longer do anything you want, but there are plenty of choices left. These further questions of language, organization, and tone often give authors great trouble because they imply commitments other than the ones already made. If you use Durkheim to discuss Marxian ideas or the language of survey research to discuss an ethnographic study, you will probably find yourself working at cross purposes. Such confusions had caused the theoretical difficulties we discovered in our copy editing exercises in the seminar.

If you start writing early in your research—before you have all your data, for instance—you can begin

cleaning up your thinking sooner. Writing a draft
without data makes clearer what you would like to
discuss and, therefore, what data you will have to get.
Writing can thus shape your research design. This
differs from the more common notion that you do your
research first and then "write it up." This extends the
Flower-Hayes (1981) idea that the early phases of
writing lead writers to see what they will have to do in
the later stages.

Making your work clearer involves considerations of
audience. Who is it supposed to be clearer to? Who will
read what you write? What do they have to know so
that they will not misread or find what you say obscure
or unintelligible? You will write one way for the people
you work with closely on a joint project, another way
for professional colleagues in your subspecialty, still
another for professional colleagues in other specialties
and disciplines, and differently yet for the "intelligent
layman."

How can you find out what readers will understand?
You can give your early drafts to sample members of
your intended audience and ask them what they think.
That is what the seminar members found so frightening
and troublesome, because showing people early drafts
exposed them to ridicule and shame. So the prescription, while simple, may not be workable. You can only
show your less-than-perfect work to people if you have
learned—as I hoped the seminar's members had from
our class exercises—that you will not be harmed if
people see it. Naturally, not everyone is a good audience for early drafts. We discovered that while editing
each other's papers. Some people, finding it difficult to
treat early drafts as early, insist on criticizing them with
the standards appropriate to finished products. Some
readers have better editorial judgment than others, and
you need a circle of people you can trust to respond
appropriately to the stage your work is in.

In addition to a theory of the act of writing, then, we
also need a theory of the social organization of writing

as a professional activity. Because most people write in absolute privacy, readers attribute the results to the author alone and credit or debit them to his or her professional reputational account. I use bookkeeping language because most people secretly think of it that way.

Why do writers work so privately? Most of them, as I said earlier, acquire their writing habits, complete with all the rituals designed to eliminate chaos and laughable results, in high school or college as adaptations to the situations in which they then write. The student's situation rewards quick, competent preparation of short, passable papers, not the skills of rewriting and redoing. (According to Woody Allen, "Eighty percent of life is getting it done and handing it in on time.") Smart students—the smarter they are, the quicker they learn—don't bother with useless skills. The first draft, being the only one, counts.

Students find the skill of writing short papers quickly less useful as they advance in graduate school. During their first few years, they may, depending on the department, have to write the same kind of papers they wrote as undergraduates. But eventually they have to write longer papers, making more complex arguments based on more complicated data. Few people can write such papers in their heads and get it right on the first try, though students may naively think that good writers routinely do. ("Getting it right" means putting the argument so clearly that the paper begins by asserting what it later demonstrates.) So students flounder, fear "getting things wrong," and don't get it done on time. Writing at the last minute, they produce papers with interesting ideas, superficial coherence, and no clear underlying argument—interesting early drafts which they nevertheless want treated as end results.

Some young sociologists (and many other young scholars as well) get into situations after graduate work that reward that style of work even less. Scholarly disciplines do not furnish such neatly marked deadlines as schools do. There are no simple "on times." Of course, there are professional "on times": if you do not publish enough articles at a rate fast enough for your department or dean, you might not be promoted or get a raise or be able to find another job. But the timetables for these productions are loose and partly shaped by administrative whim, and people may mistakenly think that more pressing concerns—preparing lectures or university service—require their immediate attention. Young scholars may thus find that time has slipped away and that they have not met a production quota less explicit than that of the undergraduate years, one they let themselves ignore because the organization did not press it on them.

Since there is no fixed time at which a paper must be submitted and no single judge who will give it a grade, scholars work on their own schedules, at their own pace. They submit the results to that amorphous body of judges, "the professional community," or at least to the representatives of that community who edit journals, make up programs for professional meetings, and give editorial opinions to book publishers. Taken together, these readers embody the diversity of opinion and practice in the discipline. That diversity makes it likely that, in the long run, authors seldom go unpublished simply because they have the wrong views or work in the wrong style. So many organizations publish so many journals that every point of view finds a home somewhere. But editors still reject papers or send them back with the instruction "revise and resubmit" because they are mixed-up—because their authors write unclearly or misstate the problem they want to address.

As a result, professional writing gets "privatized." No peer group shares the writer's problem. No group has the same paper to hand in on the same day. Everyone has a different paper to hand in whenever they get ready. So sociological writers do not develop a culture, a body of shared solutions to their shared problems. As a result, a situation that has been called pluralistic ignorance arises. Everyone thinks that everyone else is getting it done and will be ready to hand it in on time. They keep their difficulties to themselves. This may be one reason why sociologists and other scholars write in such isolation.

In any event, their work requires extensive rewriting and editorial work. Since the only version that counts is the last one, they have every reason to keep working on something until is right. Not as right as it can be, given the time available—that is the college model—but as right as they can imagine it ever being. (This, naturally, is subject to some realistic constraints, so that it will get done sometime. Remember, though, that some major works have taken twenty years to prepare and that some scholars are willing to pay the price of slow production.) But many authors don't know how to rewrite and think that every version of anything they produce will be used to judge them. (They are partly right. Such work will be used to make judgments, but if they are lucky, the judgments will be appropriate to the stage of work.) So they don't produce, or they produce in very painful ways, attempting to get whatever they put on paper into perfect form before anyone sees it.

An interesting exception to this pattern occurs in group projects where, if the work is to proceed at all, the participants must occasionally produce documents bringing each other up to date. Participants in successful projects learn to look at each other's work as preliminary, thus relieving everyone of the necessity of producing perfect drafts the first time.

More commonly, writers solve the problem of isolation by developing a circle of friends who will read their work in the right spirit, treating as preliminary what is preliminary, helping the author sort out the mixed-up ideas of a very rough draft or smooth out the ambiguous language of a later version, suggesting references that might be helpful or comparisons that will give the key to some intractable puzzle. That circle may contain friends from your graduate school cohort,

former professors, or people who share some interest.
These relationships are usually reciprocal. As the trust
between author and reader grows, the reader will ask
the author to do some reading in return. Some promis-
ing relations of this kind die when the favor isn't
returned.

Some people cannot read things in an appropriate
way. They fixate on small things—sometimes just a
word that could easily be replaced by one that avoids
the problem—and cannot think about or comment on
anything else. Others, usually known far and wide as
excellent editors, see the core problem and give helpful
suggestions. Avoid the former. Search out the latter.

The above can be read as helpful hints suggested by
the rudimentary theory of professional situations and
writing problems I have been discussing. The seminar
group, always interested in helpful hints, often lured
me into pontificating about my experience. Although
much of what I said in response to these seductions
consisted of bad imitations of Mr. Chips, a few of the
concerns are worth mentioning.

Those who had some professional experience and
had had papers rejected or sent back for extensive
revision worried about how to respond to criticism.
They frequently reverted to school talk: "Do I have to
do such and such just because they said so?" They
sometimes talked like artists whose masterwork had
been mauled by philistines. I thought they were revert-
ing to the attitude that sees most students through
college, the notion that "they" are whimsical, have no
real standards, and just decide things capriciously. If
the authorities really have no stable standards you
cannot deal with their criticisms rationally, by inspect-
ing the document you have created to see what it needs;
instead you have to find out what they want and
provide it. (See the analysis in Becker, Geer, and
Hughes 1968, 80–92.) Authors found the evidence for
this in the often contradictory advice they received

from critics: one told them to take something out while another suggested they expand the same section.

My practical tip on this point was that readers are not clairvoyant, and therefore, when an author's prose is ambiguous or confused, they don't immediately see what was really meant, but produce their own, sometimes contradictory, interpretations. A common problem arose when an author began a paper by suggesting that it was going to deal with problem X and then proceeded to analyze, in a perfectly satisfactory way, problem Y, a characteristic fault of early drafts, easily cleaned up in revision. Some critics, spotting the confusion, will suggest that the analysis, or even the research, be redone so that the paper can really deal with X. Others, more realistic, tell the author to rewrite the introduction so that it says that the paper is about Y. But critics of both kinds are responding to the same confusion. The author need not do what any of them says, but should get rid of the confusion so that it will no longer be there to complain about.

Another problem the seminar members worried about was coauthorship, and the example came out of our own class. Toward the end of the term, when we had done everything I had planned and I was at a loss for entertainments to fill the remaining seminar hours, I suggested that we write a paper together on a topic we all knew something about: problems of writing in sociology. We took turns, in a variation of an old parlor game, dictating the next sentence of the paper. Each person added to the body of the text as it grew. Some tried to follow the line suggested by their predecessors. Some ignored it and began all over again. Some made cute remarks. Several people wrote the sentences down as they were produced and read out the accumulation on request.

When we finished, we had eighteen sentences, and to everyone's surprise, despite all the non sequiturs and wisecracks, it wasn't a bad first draft, given the way we had agreed to appreciate and use first drafts. In fact, it was so interesting that I suggested we expand it for publication. That immediately raised a question: where should we publish it? We discussed the kinds of journals that might be interested in such a topic, and we finally decided on *The American Sociologist*, a journal devoted to professional problems which the American Sociological Association has unfortunately stopped publishing. I left the room to get some coffee. When I came back, the cozy atmosphere had degenerated. People were glowering at each other and confessed that they had, in my absence, begun quarreling over a predictable trouble. If some people did more work than others, who would put their names on the final paper and in what order?

I got angry at this, which was unreasonable. Many people have fought over that very real question. I told them my solution: to lean over backward and give everyone credit who conceivably might have had anything to do with it. They quickly pointed out that a tenured full professor could afford such ideas, but younger people couldn't. I don't know if they were right or not, but the idea is not foolish on its face.

We continued to talk and soon saw that only four or five students were really interested in pursuing the job. The seminar took place in the spring, and they agreed to work on it over the summer. Social organization intervened again. Graduate work is organized into classes that meet for a quarter or semester and then are over, and projects whose lives depend in some substantial way on money being available to sustain them. Since neither of these forms of automatic coordination existed beyond the end of the term during which the seminar occurred, the would-be coauthors had nothing to make them meet and continue their work, and they didn't. They never wrote the paper.

In some ways, this chapter is that paper, the residue of the work done by the participants in that class, and a lot of other people, over the last several years. When the organizations which support collective work are that ephemeral, if the work is to be done at all (and usually it isn't), one of the survivors must take it on as an individual project. Which is what has happened here.

An Afterword. I should not have said an "individual" project, because of course it wasn't. I do practice what I preach and I did send this chapter (in its original version as a stand-alone paper) to a number of people who helped me with suggestions, most of which I accepted. So my collaborators include, in addition to all the people in the three classes I have taught, the people named in the Preface.

Two

Persona and Authority

Rosanna Hertz, now a colleague but then a very advanced student, came into my office one day and said she'd like to talk to me about a chapter of her thesis-in-progress, which I had edited for her. She said, in a careful tone which I supposed hid a certain amount of irritation, that she agreed that the writing was improved—shorter, clearer, on the whole much better. But, she said, she didn't quite understand the principles that governed what I had done. Could I go over the document with her and explain them? I told her that I wasn't sure what principles governed my editorial judgment, that I really edited by ear (I'll explain that expression, which does not mean that there are no rules at all, in Chapter 4). But I agreed to do my best. I wondered whether I actually did follow any general principles of editing and thought that, if I did, I might discover them by trying to explain them to her.

Rosanna brought her chapter in a few days later. I had rewritten it extensively, cutting a lot of words but, I hoped, not losing any of her thought. It was a very good piece of work—rich data, imaginatively analyzed, well-organized—but it was very wordy and academic. I had removed as much of the redundancy and academic flourish as I thought she would stand for. We went over it, a page at a time, and she quizzed me on each point. None of my changes involved technical sociological terms. Where she wrote "unified stance" I substituted "agreement," because it was shorter. I replaced "confronted the issue" with "talked about," because it was less pretentious. A longer example: where she wrote "This chapter will examine the impact of money or, more specifically, independent incomes on relations between husbands and wives with particular regard to the realm of financial affairs," I substituted "This chapter will show that independent incomes change the way husbands and wives handle financial affairs," for similar reasons. I removed meaningless qualifications ("tends to"), combined sentences that repeated long phrases, and when she said the same thing in two ways in successive sentences, took out the less effective version, explaining what I was doing and why as I went along.

She agreed with each of my ad hoc explanations, but we weren't discovering any general principles. I asked her to take over and work on a page of text I hadn't done anything to. We went over a few lines and then came to a sentence which said that the people she was studying "could afford not to have to be concerned with" certain things. I asked how she thought she could change that. She looked and looked at the sentence and finally said that she couldn't see any way to improve that phrasing. I finally asked if she could just say that they "needn't worry" about those things.

She thought about it, set her jaw, and decided that this was the place to make her stand. "Well, yes, that is shorter, and it certainly is clearer. . . ." The thought hung unfinished as blatantly as if she had spoken the four dots aloud. After a prolonged and momentous silence, I said, "But *what?*" "Well," she said, "the other way is *classier.*"

My intuition told me the word was important. I said that she could repay all the favors she owed me by writing five pages explaining exactly what she meant when she said "classier." She looked embarrassed—it's obvious now that I was taking unfair advantage both of friendship and professorial authority—and said she would. I couldn't blame her for making me wait a couple of months for those pages. She told me later that it was the hardest thing she had ever had to write because she knew she had to tell the truth.

I am going to quote from her letter at length. But this is not just a matter of one author's character and language. "Classier" was an important clue precisely because Rosanna was saying out loud what many students and professionals in the scholarly disciplines believed and felt but, less courageous, were less willing to admit. They had hinted at what she finally wrote and the hints convinced me her attitude was widespread.

The letter I got was four double-spaced pages, and I won't quote all of it or quote it in sequence because Rosanna was thinking out loud when she wrote it and the order is not crucial. She began by remarking,

> Somewhere along the line, probably in college, I picked up on the fact that articulate people used big words, which impressed me. I remember taking two classes from a philosophy professor simply because I figured he must be really smart since I didn't know the meaning of the words he used in class. My notes from these classes are almost non-existent. I spent class time writing down the words he used that I didn't know, going home and looking them up. He sounded so smart to me simply because I didn't understand him. . . . The way someone writes—the more difficult the writing style—the more intellectual they sound.

It is no accident, as they say, that she learned to think this way in college. The excerpt expresses the perspective of a subordinate in a highly stratified organization. Colleges and universities, pretending to be communities of intellectuals who discuss matters of common interest freely and disinterestedly, are no such thing. Professors know more, have the degrees to prove it, test students and grade their papers, and in every imaginable way sit on top of the heap while students stand at the bottom. Some resent the inequality, but intelligent students who hope to be intellectuals themselves accept it wholeheartedly. They believe, like Rosanna, that the professors who teach them know more and should be imitated, whether what they do makes sense or not. The principle of hierarchy assures them that they are wrong and the teacher right. They grant the same privileges to authors:

> When I read something and I don't know immediately what it means, I always give the author the benefit of the doubt. I assume this is a smart person and the problem with my not understanding the ideas is that I'm not as smart. I don't assume either that the emperor has no clothes or that the author is not clear because of their own confusion about what they have to say. I always assume that it is my inability to understand or that there is something more going on than I'm capable of understanding. . . . I assume if it got into the *AJS* [American Journal of Sociology], for example, chances are it's good and it's important and if I don't understand it that's my problem since the journal has already legitimated it.

She makes a further point, which other people mentioned as well. (Sociologists will recognize it as a specific instance of the general problem of socialization into professional worlds, as discussed, for example, in Becker and Carper 1956a and 1956b.) Graduate students learning to be academics know that they are not real intellectuals yet—just as medical students know they are not yet real doctors—and search eagerly for signs of progress. The arcane vocabulary and syntax of stereotypical academic prose clearly distinguish lay people from professional intellectuals, just as the ability of professional ballet dancers to stand on their toes distinguishes them from ordinary folks. Learning to write like an academic moves students toward membership in that elite:

> While I personally find scholarly writing boring and prefer to spend my time reading novels, academic elitism is a part of every graduate student's socialization. I mean that academic writing is not English but written in a shorthand that only members of the profession can decipher. . . . I think it is a way to . . . maintain group boundaries of elitism. . . . Ideas are supposed to be written in such a fashion that they are difficult for untrained people to understand. This is scholarly writing. And if you want to be a scholar you need to learn to reproduce this way of writing.

(This is as good a place as any to note that, in writing the excerpts I have been quoting, Rosanna deliberately adopted a point of view she has since abandoned. When I asked her, she said that she no longer thinks that writing style has anything to do with intelligence or the complexity of ideas.)

She gave some examples of "classy" writing she had caught herself at, with explanations of why she found these locutions attractive:

> Instead of choosing to write "he lives at" I prefer "he resides at." Instead of saying "Couples spend their extra money" (or "additional money" or even "disposable income") I'd choose "surplus income." It sounds more grown-up. Here's a favorite of mine: "predicated upon the availability of" is classier than saying "exists because of" [or,

for that matter, "depends on"]. Maybe it sounds more awesome. Here's another one. I could say "domestic help" but what I choose to do is say "third party labor." The first time I use it I put a "that is" after the phrase and explain it. Then I am at liberty to use "third party labor" throughout, and it sounds fancier. I think the point here is that I am looking for a writing style that makes me sound smart.

None of these classy locutions mean anything different from the simpler ones they replace. They work ceremonially, not semantically.

Writing in a classy way to sound smart means writing to sound like, maybe even be, a certain kind of person. Sociologists, and other scholars, do that because they think (or hope) that being the right kind of person will persuade others to accept what they say as a persuasive social science argument. C. Wright Mills said that the

> lack of ready intelligibility [in scholarly writing], I believe, usually has little or nothing to do with the complexity of the subject matter, and nothing at all with profundity of thought. It has to do almost entirely with certain confusions of the academic writer about his own status. . . . In large part sociological habits of style stem from the time when sociologists had little status even with other academic men. Desire for status is one reason why academic men slip so easily into unintelligibility. . . . To overcome the academic *prose* you have first to overcome the academic *pose*. (Mills 1959, 218–19, emphasis in the original.)

Living as an intellectual or academic makes people want to appear smart, in the sense of clever or intelligent, to themselves and others. But not only smart. They also want to appear knowledgeable or worldly or sophisticated or down-home or professional—all sorts of things, many of which they can hint at in the details of their writing. They hope that being taken for such a person will make what they say believeable. We can explore what people mean when they talk or think about writing in a "classy" way, or in any other way, through the idea of a *persona* (Campbell 1975), if I can be forgiven that classy term. Although writers display their personae through the devices of style, I will not discuss style at length. Strunk and White (1959) and Williams (1981) analyze style and show writers how to use its elements effectively, and readers should pursue the subject there. (Earlier readers of this manuscript added Bernstein 1965; Follet 1966; Fowler 1965; and Shaw 1975 as useful guides to stylistic problems.) I want to emphasize how writers use personae to try get readers to accept their arguments.

Just as a Briton's accent tells listeners the speaker's class, a scholar's prose tells readers what kind of person is doing the writing. Many sociologists and other scholars, both students and professionals, want to be "classy" people, the kind of people who talk and write *that* way. Writing classy prose, they try to be or at least create the appearance of being classy.

But what is a classy person, to a young or even middle-aged scholar? My guesses about the content of these fantasies may be wrong. In fact, fantasies of classiness must vary considerably, so no one characterization will do justice to all of them. I imagine it this way: a classy person, to a young professorial type, wears a tweed jacket with leather patches at the elbow, smokes a pipe (the men, anyway), and sits around the senior common room swilling port and discussing the latest issue of the *Times Literary Supplement* or the *New York Review of Books* with a bunch of similar people. Mind you, I don't mean that the people who have these fantasies really want to be like that. The stylish young woman whose remark provoked this meditation wouldn't be caught dead in such an outfit.

But they want to talk like such a person. Perhaps not *that* person exactly, but the image gives the flavor.

Whether or not some young academics and academics-in-training want to be classy, the possibility reminds us that everyone writes as someone, affects a character, adopts a persona who does the talking for them. Literary analysts know that, but seldom examine its implications for academic writing. Academics favor a few classic personae whose traits color academic prose, shape academic arguments, and make the resulting writing more or less persuasive to various audiences. Those personae inhabit a world of scholars, researchers, and intellectuals in which it is useful or comfortable to be one or another of these people.

The academic-intellectual world has an ambiguous and uneasy relation to the ordinary world, and many academics worry about their own relation to ordinary people. Do we really differ from them enough to warrant the privileged lives we feel entitled to and often actually lead? When we claim to be thinking hard about something, although visibly just loafing in a chair, should other people let us do that? Why should we have months off from regular work "just to think?" And, especially, should anyone pay any attention to what we think? Why? The persona we adopt when we write tells readers (and by extension all the potential skeptics) who we are and why we should be believed, and that answers all the other questions.

Some personae authors adopt—general human types—deal with the problem of the relations between intellectuals and laypeople directly. Many personae emphasize the differences between us and them—our superiority in important areas—that justify our lives and show why everyone should believe us. When we present ourselves as classy, we want to see ourselves and have others see us as worldly, sophisticated, "smart" in both commonsense meanings. (Becoming an intellectual has helped enough people move up in the class system that it would be silly to ignore that meaning of "classy.") If we write in a classy way, then, we show that we are generally smarter than ordinary people, have finer sensibilities, understand things they don't, and thus should be believed.

This persona is the one that leads us to use the fancy language, big words for little ones, esoteric words for commonplace ones, and elaborate sentences making subtle distinctions that Rosanna used to find so compelling. Our language strives for the elegance we would like to embody and feel.

Other writers adopt personae which emphasize their esoteric expertise. They like to appear knowledgeable, to be the kind of person who knows "inside stuff" ordinary folks will have to wait to read about in next week's newspaper. Most specialists in matters that concern lay people in some way—labor relations, domestic politics, or perhaps some country which gets itself into the news—love to let people in on what only they know. "Inside dopesters," as David Riesman called them, let readers know who they are by a wealth of detail, mostly unexplained. They write as though their audience consisted of people who knew almost as much about it, or at least about its background— whatever it is—as they do. They mention dates, names, and places only a specialist will recognize, and don't explain. The barrage of detailed knowledge overwhelms readers, who feel compelled to accept the author's argument. How could someone who knows all that be wrong? (I have foregone including detailed examples both because they are so easily available and because each field has its own variations, which I hope readers will find and analyze for themselves.)

James Clifford has described the classic anthropological persona, invented (more or less) by Bronislaw Malinowski, which persuades the reader that the argument being made is correct because, after all, the anthropologist was there: "Malinowski gives us the imago of the new 'anthropologist'—squatting by the campfire, looking, listening and questioning, recording and interpreting Trobriand life. The literary charter of this new authority is the first chapter of *Argonauts* [*of the Western Pacific*], with its prominently displayed photographs of the ethnographer's tent pitched among the Kiriwinian dwellings" (Clifford 1983, 123).

Clifford identifies some of the stylistic devices Malinowski used to project the I-was-there persona: sixty-six photographs, a "Chronological List of Kula Events Witnessed by the Writer," and a "constant alternation between impersonal description of typical behavior and statements on the order of 'I witnessed . . .' and 'Our party, sailing from the North . . .' " He calls these devices claims to "experiential authority":

> based on a "feel" for the foreign context, a kind of accumulated savvy and sense of the style of a people or place. . . . Margaret Mead's claim to grasp the underlying principle or ethos of a culture through a heightened sensitivity to form, tone, gesture, and behavioral styles, or Malinowski's stress on his life in the village and the comprehension derived from the "imponderibilia" of daily existence are cases in point (Clifford 1983, 128).

Sociologists who do fieldwork in the anthropological style use similar devices to display a persona whose claim to authority rests on intimate knowledge. William Foote Whyte's description (1943, 14–25) of bowling with the out-of-work men he studied, known to every sociologist, is a classic example.

I gave samples of classy writing from Rosanna Hertz. It is much harder to give examples of writing that project the authoritative persona. Writing only has that character in relation to an audience. Naming the first president of the Bagel Makers' Union and giving the date of the passage of the Wagner Act will not affect a labor relations expert as it does a less specialized reader. So authoritativeness is not inherent in any piece of writing. These devices only work on an audience unfamiliar with the area. (But it might be necessary to use the same devices to convince experts that you know what you are talking about. An expert in photographic history once warned me that a paper I had written about photography would be ignored by her colleagues because I had incorrectly spelled Mathew Brady's name with two ts and Georgia O'Keeffe's with one f.)

Many academic personae make authors appear generally authoritative, entitled to the last word on whatever they are talking about. Authors who adopt these personae love to correct lay errors, to tell readers definitively what will happen in some delicate international situation whose outcome we can't imagine, to explain what "we scientists" or "we sociologists" know about things lay people have the wrong idea about.

These authorities speak in imperatives: "We must recognize . . ." "We cannot ignore . . ." They speak impersonally, talk about "one" doing things rather than using the first person. (Some grammarians think that "one" substitutes for the second person and cannot be used in place of the first person. They must never have met authorities like the ones I know.) These authorities use the passive voice to convey how little what they say depends on them personally, how much, rather, it reflects the reality their unique knowledge gives them access to. Latour and Woolgar (1979) show that laboratory scientists habitually use a typical authoritative style which conceals any traces of the ordinary human activity which produced their results. (Gusfield 1981 and Latour and Bastide 1983 explore this problem further and give additional examples.)

Some writers—I favor this persona myself—take a Will Rogers line. We are just plain folks who emphasize our similarity to ordinary people, rather than the differences. We may know a few things others don't, but it's nothing special. "Shucks, you'd of thought the same as me if you'd just been there to see what I seen. It's just that I had the time or took the trouble to be there, and you didn't or couldn't, but let me tell you about it." Something like that. (In fact, this whole book is an extended example of that persona.)

Such writers want to use their similarity to others, their ordinariness, to persuade readers that what they are saying is right. We write more informally, favor the personal pronoun, and appeal to what we-and-the-reader know in common rather than what we know and the reader doesn't.

Every style, then, is the voice of someone the author wants to be, or be taken for. I haven't explored all the types here, and a proper study would begin with a thorough analysis of the major voices in which academics and intellectuals write. That ambitious study is more than this book needs. (A number of social scientists have begun the job. In addition to Clifford 1983, see Geertz 1983 on anthropology and McCloskey 1983 and McCloskey in an unpublished paper on economics.)

This analysis of personae may suggest that there is something illegitimate about speaking in any of these ways. Clearly, you can use these devices illegitimately, to disguise inadequacies of evidence or argument. But we will often, quite reasonably if not logically, accept an argument in part just because the author clearly knows the field (including presidents of the Bagel Makers' Union) or has a general cultural sophistication we respect. The author can't be nobody, so every author will necessarily be somebody. It might as well be someone readers respect and believe.

The list of available personae varies among academic disciplines, because one source of personae is famous teachers or characters in a field. Admiring their teachers, students imitate not only their personal mannerisms, but also the way they write, especially when that style projects a distinctive personality. Thus, many philosophers adopted the diffident, tentative, arrogant persona and the worrying, conversational prose style of

Ludwig Wittgenstein, just as many sociologists who took up ethnomethodology decorated their papers with the endless lists and qualifications of its founder, Harold Garfinkel.

Imitating teachers is the specific form of a general tendency to indicate theoretical and political allegiances by the way one writes. Scholars worry a lot about which "school" they belong to, with good reason, for many fields, highly factionalized, reward and punish people by the allegiances they display. Disciplines seldom do that as rigorously or ruthlessly as authors think, but nervous scholars do not wholly imagine the dangers. You can easily demonstrate your allegiances by using a school's code words, which differ from the words adherents of other schools use, in part, because the theories they belong to in fact give them a slightly different meaning. Most sociological theories rely, for instance, on the idea that people remake society continuously by doing, day in and day out, the things that reaffirm that that is the way things are done. You might say that people create society by acting as though it existed. You might say, if you were a Marxist theorist, that people reproduce social relations through daily practice. If you were a symbolic interactionist, or an adherent of Berger and Luckmann, you might speak of the social construction of reality.

These are not just different words. They express different thoughts. Still, not that different. Code words don't always contain a core of unique meaning, but we still want to use them rather than some other words that might lead people to think that we belong, or would like to belong, to some other school to. The allegiance-signalling purpose of stylistic devices is clearest when the author says things that conflict with the theory the language signals, when the desire to say "I am a functionalist" or "I am a Marxist" overcomes the desire to say what you mean. (Stinchcombe elaborates this idea in an article cited and discussed in Chapter 8.)

John Walton, reading an earlier version of this material and thinking over his experience teaching a seminar something like mine, points out that often

> People want very much to show their theoretical colors, to signal to the hip reader (professor or editor) that they are on the right side of a controversial issue. I see that most with writing that wants to communicate sophisticaton in Marxism without appearing as orthodoxy or susceptible to being branded as such. A term like "social formation" dropped in the right place says what you want to other sophisticates, without carrying much risk.

Walton puts an important point into that parenthesis—that we want to signal somebody in particular, not an abstraction. Whom we want to signal depends on the arena we are operating in, and arenas are often more local than scholarly writers realize, particularly for students. The sociologists and other professors I see in Chicago have different worries and make different criticisms than those Walton sees in Davis, California, and we both have larger professional audiences which differ as well.

Remember that academic writers take on many allegiances to schools and political positions while still in graduate school. That accounts for another major source of stylistic problems. When I argued with students about how they wrote—when I suggested to Rosanna that she write in a way she thought not classy—they told me that I was wrong because that *was* the way sociologists wrote. I spent a lot of time arguing about that before I saw their point.

The point is professionalization. Academics-in-training worry about whether they are yet, can ever be, or even want to be professional intellectuals of the kind they are changing themselves into. Second or third or fourth year graduate students have not taken binding vows. They may have second thoughts. Nor have they been finally chosen. They might flunk out. Their committee might turn their theses down. Who knows what might happen?

That uncertainty creates another reason (beyond those discussed earlier) for magical thinking and practice. If you act as though you already were a sociologist, you might fool everyone into accepting you as one, and even take it seriously yourself. Writing is one of the few ways a graduate student can act like a professional. Just as medical students can only do a few of things real doctors routinely do, graduate students do not become professionals until they get their Ph.D. degrees. Until then, they can teach as graduate assistants and work on other people's projects, but will not be taken as seriously as people with degrees. At least, they think that's true, and they are mostly right, so they adopt what they see around them, the style professional journal articles and books are written in, as an appropriate signal of their guild membership.

What kind of writing will do that for them? Not writing plain English prose. Anyone can do that. Students share the attitudes of many art audiences toward "ordinary" modes of expression:

> Artistic innovators frequently try to avoid what they regard as the excessive formalism, sterility, and hermeticism of their medium by exploiting the actions and objects of everyday life. Choreographers like Paul Taylor and Brenda Way use running, jumping, and falling down as conventionalized dance movements, instead of the more formal movements of classical ballet, or even of traditional modern dance. . . . [But] less involved audiences look precisely for the conventional formal elements the innovators replace to distinguish art from nonart. They do not go to the ballet to see people run, jump, and fall down; they can see that anywhere. They go instead to see people do the difficult and esoteric formal movements

that signify "real dancing." The ability to see
ordinary material as art material—to see that the
running, jumping, and falling down are not just
that, but are the elements of a different language of
the medium—thus distinguishes serious audience
members from the well-socialized member of the
culture, the irony being that these materials are
perfectly well known to the latter, although not as
art materials (Becker 1982a, 49–50).

Students are like that. They know plain English but
don't want to use it to express their hard-earned knowledge. Remember the student who said, "Gee, Howie, if
you say it that way it sounds like something anyone
could say." If you want to convince yourself that the
time and effort spent getting your degree are worth it,
that you are changing in some way that will change
your life, then you want to look different from everyone
else, not the same. That accounts for a truly crazy cycle
in which students repeat the worst stylistic excesses
the journals contain, learn that those very excesses are
what makes their work different from what every damn
fool knows and says, write more articles like those they
learned from, submit them to journals whose editors
publish them because nothing better is available (and
because academic journals cannot afford expensive
copy editing) and thus provide the raw material for
another generation to learn bad habits from.

I thought the idea that "they" made you write that
way was only student paranoia. When I published
chapter 1 in The Sociological Quarterly, the editors
received a letter which made some of the same points:

We suggest that a new voice, an "unknown" in
the field today has to earn the "respect" of the
profession through a compilation of notable research and traditional writing before s/he receives
the license to adopt the direct, uncluttered style
advocated by Becker. Some journal editors may be
"licensed" to use this style, and thus receptive to

it, by the time they achieve editorial positions; however, the receptiveness of editors may be a moot point since most journals are refereed. Perhaps some referees are receptive to this writing style, but perhaps most are not. Articles that are verbose, pretentious, and dull still abound in sociology. . . . We question the wisdom of advising students and faculty just entering the world of "publish or perish" to abandon the ponderous, rigid style of the discipline. . . . Currently, and in the probable future, graduate students . . . will "learn" to write by reading what is written. They generally find dull, verbose, pretentious writing, perpetuating the problem and suggesting that most referees expect such a stilted style (Hummel and Foster 1984, 429–31 [my emphasis]).

Three

One Right Way

Scholarly writers have to organize their material, express an argument clearly enough that readers can follow the reasoning and accept the conclusions. They make this job harder than it need be when they think that there is only One Right Way to do it, that each paper they write has a preordained structure they must find. They simplify their work, on the other hand, when they recognize that there are many effective ways to say something and that their job is only to choose one and execute it so that readers will know what they are doing.

I have a lot of trouble with students (and not just students) when I go over their papers and suggest revisions. They get tongue-tied and act ashamed and upset when I say that this is a good start, all you have to do is this, that, and the other and it will be in good shape. Why do they think there is something wrong with changing what they have written? Why are they so leery of rewriting?

It might be laziness. You might decide (chapter 9 discusses this) that it is physically too much trouble to do it again. You just don't feel like retyping a page or cutting-and-pasting any more.

More often, students and scholars balk at rewriting because they are subordinates in a hierarchical organization, usually a school. The master-servant or boss-worker relationship characteristic of schools gives people a lot of reasons for not wanting to rewrite, many of them quite sensible. Teachers and administrators intend their schools' systems of reward to encourage learning. But those systems usually teach undergraduates, instead, to earn grades rather than to be interested in the subjects they study or to do a really good job. (This discussion is based on the research reported in Becker, Geer, and Hughes 1968.) Students try to find out, by interrogating instructors and relying on the experience of other students, exactly what they have to do to get good grades. When they find out, they do what they have learned is necessary, and no more. Few students learn (and here we can rely on our own memories as students and teachers) that they have to rewrite or revise anything. On the contrary, they learn that a really smart student does a paper once, making it as good as possible in one pass. If you really don't care very much about the work you are doing—if it is just a chore to be done for a course, and you have calculated that it is worth only so much effort and no more—then you might reasonably do it once and to hell with it. You have better ways to spend your time.

Schools also teach students to think of writing as a kind of test: the teacher hands you the problem, and you try to answer it, then go on to the next problem. One shot per problem. Going over it is, somehow, "cheating," especially when you have had the benefit of someone else's coaching after your first try. It's somehow no longer a fair test of your own abilities. You can hear your sixth grade teacher saying, "Is this all your own work?" What a student might think of as

coaching and cheating, of course, is what more experienced people think of as getting some critical response
from informed readers.

Joseph Williams suggested to me that students, being
young, simply don't have the experience of life that
would let them use their imaginations to get out of their
own egocentric worlds. They thus cannot imagine an
audience's response or the possibility of a text other
than the one they have already produced. That may be
true. But the lack of experience may result less from
youth than from the way schools infantilize young
people. Graduate students certainly appreciate the
need for rewriting more keenly when, contemplating
reading their paper at a professional meeting, they
envision total strangers assaulting their logic, evidence,
and prose.

Such reasons might explain why people don't rewrite, but not the shame and embarrassment they feel at
the thought of doing it. These feelings also originate in
schools. No one connected with schools, neither teachers nor administrators, tells students how the writing
they read—textbooks or their own teachers' research
reports, for instance—actually gets done. In fact, as I
said earlier (citing Latour, Shaughnessy, and others),
the separation of scholarly work from teaching in
almost all schools hides the process from students. (Just
as, according to Thomas Kuhn, histories of science hide
all the false turns and mistakes in the research programs that produced the successes they celebrate.)
Students don't know, never seeing their teacher, let
alone textbook authors, at work, that all these people do
things more than once, rather than treating their professional work as a quasi-test. Students don't know that
journal editors routinely send papers back for revision,
that publishers hire editors to improve the prose of
books to be published. They don't know that revising
and editing happen to everyone, and are not emergency
procedures undertaken only in cases of scandalously
unprofessional incompetence.

Students think of their teachers, and the textbook authors their teachers stand for, as authorities for another obvious reason: these people stand above them in the school hierarchy. They are the bosses who give the grades and judge whether students' work is good enough. Unless students decide that the educational institutions they attend are frauds (and surprisingly few do, considering the evidence available to them), they will accept the implicit organizational proposition that the people who run schools know what they are doing. Not only, then, do their academic superiors—as far as they can see—never rewrite anything, they also get what they write "right" the first time. So students learn and really believe, at least for a while, that "real writers" (or "professionals" or "smart people") get it right the first time. Only dummies have to do it over and over. This might be another version of the test mentality: the ability to do it right the first time shows superior ability. This, too, is hierarchy, full-blown, at its worst: subordinates taking such evaluations as grades and teachers' comments, which are legitimated by the stratification of schools and scholarship, as ultimate and not-to-be-questioned evaluations of their own personal worth. (Becker, Geer and Hughes 1968, 116–128, detail the evidence for this interpretation.)

All these ideas—about not rewriting, about the school paper as a sign of worth—rest on the fallacious premise that there is a "right answer," a "best way" to do things. Some readers will think I have invented a strawman, that serious students and scholars know there is no One Right Way. But students and scholars do believe in One Right Way, because the institutions they work in embody that idea. The ideas of the right answer and a best way find their natural home in hierarchy. Most people believe that the higher-ups in hierarchical organizations know more and know better than the people lower down. They don't. Studies of organizations show that superiors may know more about some things, but usually know a good deal less

about many others. They even know less about the
organization's central business, which you might suppose they would know better. But the official theory of
the organization, and usually of its environing society,
ignores such results, holding that higher-ups really do
know better. What they know is, in fact, by definition
the "right answer."

No matter that real authorities on any subject know
that there is never one right answer, just a lot of
provisional answers competing for attention and ac-
ceptance. Students, undergraduates particularly, don't
like such talk. Why bother learning something that isn't
true only to have to learn something else in its place
tomorrow? Nor do true-believing scholars like it,
whether they have discovered the truth themselves, or
are only followers of the discoverers. The leaders of the
field must know. What they know is what's in the book.
That is real hierarchy, seen most clearly when a chem-
istry experiment performed in class fails to produce the
"correct" result and the teacher tells students what
should have happened and what, therefore, they
should write in their notebooks. (Yes, that does happen.)

If there is one right answer, and you believe that the
authorities who run the institution you work in know
it, then you know that your job is to find out the right
answer and reproduce it when required, thus showing
that you deserve to be rewarded, maybe even to become
one of the guardians yourself. That is the undergraduate version. A slightly more sophisticated version afflicts graduate students and professionals. Since what
you are writing is something new, the One Right Way
does not exist, but its Platonic ideal exists somewhere
and it is up to you to discover it and put it down on
paper. I suppose that many of us would like readers to
feel that we have found such a preordained right way to
say what we say, one that looks as though it could only
be that way. But serious writers discover that perfect
form (that is, some form that does what they want done,

even though not the only possible one) after lengthy exploration, not the first time.

Harvey Molotch put the point like this in a note to me:

> A problem that writing people have is the idea in their heads that a given sentence, paragraph or paper must be the *right* one. Their training in a land of "facts," in the celebration of "right answers"—including the "right" way to approach their Chem lab book or English theme—immobilizes them at the typewriter keyboard. Their problem is that there are many right sentences, many right structures for an essay. . . . We have to free ourselves from the idea that there is only one CORRECT way. When we don't, the contradiction with reality absolutely stifles us since no sentence, paragraph or paper is demonstrable (to ourselves) as clearly the right one. Students watch their words come out, but of course these words— in first draft—are not even meeting the test of "OK," much less CORRECT and PERFECT ESSENCE OF CORRECT. Not having a vision of tentativeness, of first-draft, of n-draft, they can only feel frustration at the sight of failure. After a while, one sees the first tentative *thoughts* of a paragraph or paper as obviously failing this test— and so one doesn't even start: writer's cramp. The fear of failure is an *accurate* fear, because *nobody* could pass this self-imposed test of getting the one correct version, and the failure to do so is especially (and distressingly) evident at the point of first-draft.

Some very common, quite specific writing difficulties have their origins in this attitude: the problem of getting started and the problem of "which way to organize it." Neither one has a unique solution to be discovered. Whatever you do will be a compromise between conflicting possibilities. That doesn't mean that you can't arrive at workable solutions, only that you can't count on finding the one perfect one that was there all along waiting to be found.

Most writers, even professionals, have trouble getting started. They start over and over again, destroying reams of paper, working over the first sentence or paragraph again and again as they find each successive try unsatisfactory in some new way. They start that way because they believe that there is One Right Way. If they can only find the Right Way to begin, they think, everything else will take care of itself, all the other problems that they fear are lurking ahead of them will disappear. They set themselves up to fail.

Suppose I am reporting on my study of Chicago schoolteachers. (I have immodestly used this ancient document, my own Ph.D. thesis, as an example because I know it well, and because the problems it exemplifies still bother students, who find the solutions I discuss helpful.) The study dealt with, loosely speaking, race, class, professional culture, and institutional organization. How shall I begin? I could say: "Schoolteacher culture defines lower-class, and especially black, students as difficult to work with. As a result, teachers avoid those schools, transferring to higher-class schools as soon as their seniority makes it possible, and that in turn means that lower-class schools are always staffed by new, inexperienced teachers." Even though I am talking about a thesis completed and accepted in 1951, I still have trouble writing a concise introductory sentence. (Imagine me trying to do it in 1951, when I still wasn't sure what the thesis was about.) When I look at the sentence I just typed, I might think, "Wait a minute, do I *really* want to say 'schoolteacher culture'? After all, it's not exactly culture in the strict anthropological sense, is it? I mean, they don't pass it on from generation to generation, and it doesn't cover all aspects of life, isn't really a 'design for living.' If I call it culture, I'm sure to get in trouble, and I'll deserve it, because I will be saying something I might not mean." So I put that sheet in the wastebasket, and try again.

I might substitute "shared beliefs" for "culture" and feel happier with that. But then I would see that I was talking about class and remember what a tangle of implications surrounds every one of the many ways sociologists talk about class. Whose version would I mean? W. Lloyd Warner's? Karl Marx's? I might decide to go back over the literature on class again before using such an expression. So I would put another sheet in the typewriter. But now I might notice that I had said "As a result of something teachers something-or-other." That is a pretty direct causal statement. Do I really think that social causality works like that? Shouldn't I use some less committing expression? In short, every way to say it would start me down some path I hadn't fully explored and might not want to take if I really understood what it would commit me to. The simplest remarks would have implications I might not like, and I wouldn't even know I was implying them. (Curious readers can see what I actually did by consulting Becker 1980.)

That is why people make outlines. Maybe working the whole puzzle out in outline will show you where you are going, help you catch all the implications, evade all the traps, and get it all to come out right. You will find the One Right Way. An outline can help you get started, even if it won't find the Way, but only if it is so detailed as to be the actual paper whose skeleton it pretends to be. That just gives you the same problem in a slightly different form.

Introductions raise the problem of unwanted implications in a specially difficult way. Everett Hughes told me, when I was still in graduate school, to write introductions last. "Introductions are supposed to introduce. How can you introduce something you haven't written yet? You don't know what it is. Get it written and then you can introduce it." If I do that, I discover that I have a variety of possible introductions available, each one *right* in some way, each giving a slightly different twist to my thought. I don't have to find the

One Right Way to say what I want to say; I have to find
out what I want to say. But I can do that more easily
after I have said it all and know pretty much what I
mean than when I am writing the first sentence. If I
write my introductory sentences after I finish the body
of my text, the problem of the One Right Way is less
compelling.

Fearing commitment to the implications of an initial
formulation also accounts for people beginning with
the vacuous sentences and paragraphs so common in
scholarly writing. "This study deals with the problem
of careers" or "Race, class, professional culture, and
institutional organization all affect the problem of public education." Those sentences employ a typical evasive maneuver, pointing to something without saying
anything, or anything much, about it. *What* about
careers? How do all those things affect public education? People who make outlines do the same thing by
making topic rather than sentence outlines. The minute
you turn the topic headings into nonvacuous sentences, the problems the outline solved return.

Many social scientists, however, think they are actually doing a good thing by beginning evasively. They
reveal items of evidence one at a time, like clues in a
detective story, expecting readers to keep everything
straight until they triumphantly produce the dramatic
concluding paragraph that summarizes argument and
evidence at once. They may do this out of a scientific
prudery which forbids stating a conclusion before laying out all the evidence (which ignores the excellent
example of mathematical proofs that begin by stating
the proposition to be proved). Investigators frequently
report survey research results this way. A table shows,
for example, that class and racial prejudice are directly
related. The next table shows that that is true only
when you hold education constant. Further tables
showing the effect of age or ethnicity complicate matters further, and so on down a long road of items before

whatever conclusion the assemblage warrants finally appears.

I often suggest to these would-be Conan Doyles that they simply put their last triumphant paragraph first, telling readers where the argument is going and what all this material will finally demonstrate. That flushes out the other reason for this caginess: "If I give the ending away at the beginning, no one will read the rest of what I've written." But scientific papers seldom deal with material suspenseful enough to warrant the format. If you put the paragraph that gives the secret away at the beginning, you can then go back and say explicitly what each section of your work contributes to reaching that result, instead of having to hide its function in noncommittal prose.

Suppose you are reporting, as Prudence Rains (1971) did, the results of a study of unwed mothers. You *could*, in classical evasive style, begin your book like this: "This study investigates the experiences of unwed mothers, with special attention to their careers, moral aspects of their situations, and the influence of social agencies." Giving nothing at all away, that beginning would leave the reader with a collection of unrelated tokens to be exchanged later in the book (if the author delivers on the I.O.U.) for sentences asserting real relationships between real entities.

Fortunately, Rains did not do that. She wrote, instead, a model introduction, which explains exactly what the rest of the book then analyzes in detail. I quote it at length:

> Becoming an unwed mother is the outcome of a particular sequence of events that begins with forays into intimacy and sexuality, results in pregnancy, and terminates in the birth of an illegitimate child. Many girls do not have sexual relations before marriage. Many who do, do not get pregnant. And most girls who get pregnant while unmarried do not end up as unwed mothers. Girls

who become unwed mothers, in this sense, share a common career that consists of the steps by which they came to be unwed mothers rather than brides, the clients of abortionists, contraceptively prepared lovers, or virtuous young ladies.

The most significant aspects of this career are moral ones, for sexuality, pregnancy, and motherhood are matters closely linked to conceptions of feminine respectability and intimately connected to women's conceptions of themselves. Becoming an unwed mother is not simply a private and practical trouble; it is the kind of trouble that forces public accounting, raises retrospective questions, and, above all, calls into question the kind of person the unwed mother was and is.

The moral career of an unwed mother is, in this sense, like the moral careers of other persons whose acts are treated as deviant, and whose selves become publicly implicated. Important, if not central, to the moral career of such a person are the social agencies with which he may come into contact as a result of his situation. Social agencies and institutions, whether geared to rehabilitation, incarceration, help, or punishment, provide and enforce interpretations of the person's current situation, of the past that led to it, and of the possibilities that lie ahead (Rains 1971, 1–2.).

That introduction, laying out the map of the trip the author is going to take them on, lets readers connect any part of the argument with its overall structure. Readers with such a map seldom get confused or lost.

Evasive vacuous sentences, however, are actually good ways to begin early drafts. They give you some leeway at a time when you don't want or need to be committed, and most important, they let you start. Write one down and you can go ahead without worrying that you have put your foot on a wrong path, because you haven't really taken a step yet. You just have to remember, when you have written the rest of what you have to say, to go back and replace these placeholders with real sentences that say what you mean.

Suppose I take this advice and start somewhere else. If I don't begin at the beginning, where do I begin? What do I write first? Won't anything I write commit me as much as a first sentence? Doesn't every sentence somehow contain in itself, at least by implication, the whole argument? Sure. So what? Remember that any sentence can be changed, rewritten, thrown out or contradicted. That lets you write anything at all. No sentence commits, not because it doesn't prefigure your argument in just the way people fear, but because nothing bad will happen if it is wrong. You can write utter nonsense, things that turn out not to be what you think at all, and nothing will happen. Try it.

Once you know that writing a sentence down won't hurt you, know it because you have tried it, you can do what I usually ask people to try: write whatever comes into your head, as fast as you can type, without reference to outlines, notes, data, books or any other aids. The object is to find out what you would like to say, what all your earlier work on the topic or project has already led you to believe. (I here "invented", as I mentioned earlier, the device known to teachers of composition as "freewriting," which is described fully in Elbow 1981, 13–19.)

If you can bring yourself to do this (Pamela Richards discusses the reasons for not doing it in chapter 6), you will make some interesting discoveries. If you follow the directions and write whatever comes into your head, you will find that you do not have the bewildering variety of choices you feared. You can see, once you have your work on paper, that most of it consists of slight variations on a very few themes. You do know what you want to say and, once you have the different versions before you, you can easily see how trivial the differences are. Or if there are real differences (though there seldom are), you now know what your choices are.

(The same trick helps students who get hung up trying to frame a dissertation topic. I ask them to write down, in no more than one or two sentences, one hundred different thesis ideas. Few people get past twenty or twenty-five before they see that they only have two or three ideas, which are almost always variations on a common theme.)

If you write this way, you usually find out, by the time you get to the end of your draft, what you have in mind. Your last paragraph reveals to you what the introduction ought to contain, and you can go back and put it in and then make the minor changes in other paragraphs your new-found focus requires.

In short, by the time we come to write something, we have done a lot of thinking. We have an investment in everything we have already worked out that commits us to a point of view and a way of handling the problem. We probably couldn't, even if we wanted to, handle the problem any differently from the way we will end up handling it. We are committed, not by the choice of a word, but by the analysis we have already done. That's why it makes no difference how we begin. We chose our path and destination long before.

Writing an unthought-out, unplanned draft (what Joy Charlton once inelegantly but accurately called a "spew" draft) demonstrates something else. You can't deal with the welter of thoughts that flash through your head when you sit at your keyboard trying to think where to begin. No one can. The fear of that chaos is one reason for the rituals the students in my seminar described. First one thing, then another, comes into your head. By the time you have thought the fourth thought, the first one is gone. For all you know, the fifth thought is the same as the first. In a short time, certainly, you have gone through your whole repertoire. How many thoughts can we have on one topic?

> Trying to evaluate, elaborate, and relate all that
> we know on a given topic can easily overload the
> capacity of our working memory. Trying to com-
> pose even a single sentence can have the same
> effect, as we try to juggle grammatical and syntac-
> tical alternatives plus all the possibilities of tone,
> nuance, and rhythm even a simple sentence of-
> fers. Composing, then, is a cognitive activity that
> constantly threatens to overload short-term mem-
> ory. (Flower 1979, 36)

That's why it is so important to write a draft rather
than to keep on preparing and thinking about what you
will write when you do start. (Joseph Williams suggests
reserving the word draft for the first version that aims at
coherence, to emphasize that freewriting produces a
collection of working notes that shouldn't be mistaken
for something more organized.) You need to give the
thoughts a physical embodiment, *to put them down on
paper*. A thought written down (and not immediately
thrown into the wastebasket) is stubborn, doesn't
change its shape, can be compared with the other
thoughts that come after it. You can only learn how few
thoughts you really have if you write them all down, set
them side by side and compare them. That's one reason
why dictating an early draft onto tape, even if you do
the transcription yourself, is useful. You can't throw
away a page of a tape very easily; you can still erase a
foolish thought, but it is a lot of trouble, and most
people find it easier just to keep talking and make
changes on a typed version. Making the words physically real, then, does not commit you to dangerous
positions. Just the opposite. It makes sorting out your
thoughts easier. It makes writing the first sentences
easier by letting you see what you want to say.

Using the language of cognitive psychology, Flower
and Hayes 1979, describe a similar process of working
back from written materials to a plan and then forward
to another piece of writing. The paper deals with a

much smaller project—writing a short theme over the course of a few minutes, rather than a scholarly paper or book over a period of months or years—but the discussion of how writers create elaborate networks of goals and sub-goals and change their high-level goals in the light of what they have learned by writing is relevant to our discussion.

A problem as insoluble as how to begin—another version of it, in fact—is how to organize what you have to say. Students often complain that they can't decide how to organize their material, whether to say this or that first, whether to use this idea as an organizing principle or that one. The theory of One Right Way to do things causes mischief here too. Another example from my thesis will provide material for the analysis.

I had simple results to report. Schoolteachers evaluated a number of aspects of their job: their relationships with the students they taught, the students' parents, the principal they worked for, and the other teachers they worked with. They liked those people in each category who made their work easier, disliked those who made it harder. In their view, schools varied most importantly in the social class of their students. They found slum children difficult to teach; they found upper-middle class students difficult too, smart but not respectful enough of the teacher's age and authority. Most teachers preferred working-class children, who could do ordinary schoolwork but were docile and thus easy to handle. They also preferred working-class parents, who were most helpful in controlling their own children. Residential segregation made distinguishing schools by students' social class easy to do. Most schools were predominantly one or another class.

That analysis gave me a simple choice of ways of organizing my material (which came from sixty interviews with teachers.) I could analyze, in turn, the relations teachers had with students, parents, principals, and other teachers, describing under each heading how those relations varied depending on the social class of the school. Or I could write in turn about slum schools, working-class schools, and upper-middle-class schools, explaining the particular constellation of teachers' relations with those four groups that characterized schools of each class.

How did I choose? I couldn't see that it made any difference, at least with respect to the bulk of the writing I had to do. Whichever way I chose, I would have to describe teachers and working-class kids, teachers and slum school colleagues, teachers and the principals of middle-class schools, and all the other combinations of relations and school types created by cross-classifying relation and class. My smallest descriptive units, analyzing those combinations, would be the same. The opening and closing sentences, relating the smaller units to the whole, would be different, as would the final arguments I made. But I would be able to use whatever I wrote, however I finally put the material together. Either way, I would report the same results (although in a different order) and arrive at essentially the same conclusions (though the terms they were put in and their emphases would differ). What I said about the implications for social science theory and social policy would differ, naturally. If I used my results to answer different questions, the answers would look different. But none of that would affect the work that lay immediately ahead of me as I began writing my thesis. Why worry about it?

I worried about it—everyone worries about it—because the problem, while very important, can't be solved rationally. Whichever way I chose, I found myself wanting to talk about, or talking about, something I hadn't mentioned or explained yet. I could start by talking about slum schools, but only if I talked about the four groups and teachers' relations with them. But I couldn't talk about those relations without explaining the theoretical issues involved. I would have to explain, for instance, that service workers, like teachers, typically judge people they work with on the basis of

how easy or difficult those people make it to get
through a day's work. If I did that, I would be starting
with the relations. But I couldn't say anything sensible
about the relations without first explaining social class
and its bearing on children's ability to learn school
materials and to behave in ways acceptable to teachers,
and on parents' willingness and ability to help teachers
keep children in line. You can see where that leads.

It once led my colleague Blanche Geer to wish for a
way to write what she had to say on the surface of a
sphere, so that nothing would have to come first. That
would shift the problem of what to take up first to the
reader. The image of writing on a sphere exactly captures the insoluble nature of the problem, as people
usually define it. You can't talk about everything at
once, no matter how much you want to, no matter how
much it seems to be the only way. You can, of course,
solve the problem. Everyone eventually does. You do it
by taking up, for instance, the relations between the
teachers and other groups and saying that there is also
this other way of looking at it, and in due time you will
explain that too. This is not so much a placeholder as
an I.O.U.

Writers find the question of which-way-to-organize-
it a problem, again, because they imagine that one of
the ways is Right. They don't let themselves see that
each of the several ways they can think of has something to recommend it, that none are perfect. Believers
in Platonic perfection don't like pragmatic compro-
mises and accept them only when reality—the need to
finish a paper or thesis, for instance—compels it.

But writers have more immediate reasons to worry
than not knowing the One Right Way. They don't even
know, at the beginning, what those smallest units are,
the fragments out of which the final result will be made.
Another is that they don't have much idea about the
alternate ways they might be put together. They don't,
for instance, know that they can choose between organizing their discussion around kinds of schools or

kinds of work relations. They have vague notions that one thing might lead to another, that one idea might stand in a causal relation of some sort to another, that one idea is a specific version of another more general one. But they might be wrong. Those ideas might contradict something they read in Durkheim or Weber, conflict with the results of someone else's research, or even be belied by their own data. People hope to solve these problems by making outlines.

Outlines can help, but not if you begin with them. If you begin, instead, by writing down *everything*, by spewing out your ideas as fast as you can type, you will discover the answer to the first question: the fragments you have to work with are the various things you have just written. These fragments will be at every level of generality or should be. Some will be specific observations: teachers hate kids who talk dirty. Some will be more general: teachers can't stand anyone challenging their authority in the classroom. Some will relate to the scholarly literature: Max Weber says that bureaucracy is a rule of secret sessions. Some will be about social organization: slum schools have unstable teacher populations, while upper-middle class schools, because teachers seldom leave them, have more stable teaching staffs. Some will be about careers and individual experience: teachers who, for whatever reason, have spent several years in a slum school, no longer want to leave it.

Once you have the fragments, you can see how disparate they are, how they range from the general to the particular and don't seem to stick to any one way of thinking about your topic. Now you have to arrange them so that they at least seem to move logically from point to point in what a reader would recognize as a reasonable argument. How can you do that?

People solve this problem in a variety of ways. I use this principle to choose among possible solutions: Do whatever is easiest first. Write the part that is easiest to write, do simple housekeeping chores like sorting your papers out. (A contradictory approach regards any task that is easy suspect and tries, rather, to start with what is hardest. I don't recommend that kind of Puritanism.) Here is one easy way to discover how to organize your materials. Its greatest virtue (and this is a corollary of the principle of doing easy things first) is that it transforms a difficult mental task into a largely physical, and therefore easier, one.

Begin by taking notes on what you have written, putting each idea on a file card. Don't discard any of the ideas in your draft. They may come in handy, even if you can't see how at the moment; your subconscious knows things you don't. Now sort your stack of cards into piles. Put the ones that seem to go together in one pile. "Seem to go together?" Yes, and don't look too closely, for the moment, for what they have in common. Follow your intuition. When you have assembled these piles, make a card to go on top of each one, a card that summarizes what all the cards in the pile say, generalizing their particulars. For the first time you can begin to be critical of what you have done. If you can't think of a statement that covers all the cards in the pile, take out the ones that don't fit and make new piles for them, with their own summary cards. Now lay your generalization cards out on a table or on the floor, or pin them up on the wall (I got the pinning-on-the-wall habit from working with photographs, which photographers ordinarily inspect by leaving them pinned up for a week or two). Lay them out in some order, any order. Maybe you can make a linear order in which one idea leads to another. Maybe you can lay some of them out in a column, one under the other, which would physically indicate a relation of specific example or subargument to more general statement.

You will soon see that there is more than one way, but not very many more, to make your case. The ways are not identical, because they emphasize different parts of your analysis. If I organize my analysis of schoolteachers around kinds of schools, I will emphasize the local social organization of the school and to some degree lose the comparative emphasis on professional problems that an analysis focused on the relations would emphasize. This way of experimenting with the organization of ideas has been somewhat formalized in the idea of the *flow chart*. Walter Buckley provided a good example in his formalization of Thomas Scheff's theory of mental illness. The chart, reproduced here as figure 1, comes from Buckley (1966). You needn't know the theory involved to see how this device clarifies an argument.

Doing all these things, by the way, helps solve another common "minor" problem. Social scientists reporting empirical research always include a descriptive section, telling something about the country, town, or organization they did their research in. What should such sections include? Researchers vaguely intend them to give readers "a feel for the place," and fill them from a commonly accepted list of things every reader would presumably need to know, a mélange of geography, demography, history, and organization charts. Writing enough to know what your argument is helps you make the choice more rationally.

The facts about places, people, and organization do more than give readers a general familiarity. Social organizations work the way the research report says they do only with the right kinds of people and in the right kinds of places. So preliminary descriptive materials set down some of the basic premises on which the report's argument rests. If our book (Becker, Geer and Hughes 1968, 15 ff.) describes a student culture which profoundly affects student lives and perspectives, the reader needs to know that the college we are talking about is, for instance, large and that it is, in fact, the dominant institution in a small midwestern town, and that a large number of the students come from smaller, less cosmopolitan places.

I find one further way of dealing with organizational problems interesting. Instead of trying to solve the

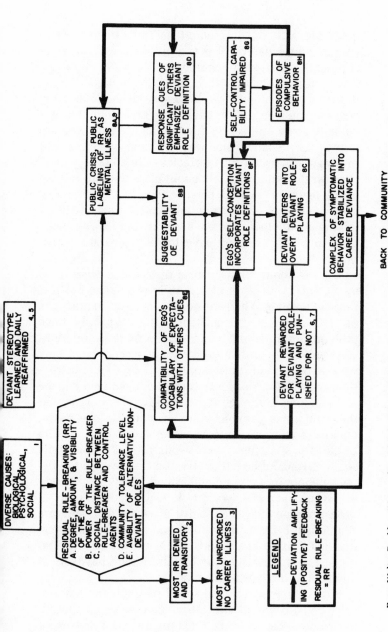

From Walter Buckley, "Appendix: A Methodological Note," in Thomas Scheff, *Being Mentally Ill* (Chicago: Aldine, 1966).

insoluble, you can talk about it. You can explain to readers why whatever it is is a problem, what ways of solving it you have thought about, why you chose the less-than-perfect solution you actually chose, and what it all means. The what-it-all-means will be interesting because you wouldn't be having the problem if it didn't embody some interesting dilemma in the work you are doing—for instance, the way problems of class and professional structure intersect in concrete organizations so that you can't talk about class without talking about teachers' shared perspectives on their professional relations, and can't talk about those without talking about class. You have trouble only if you insist that, in principle, they have to be discussable separately.

Talking about them, instead of trying to wish them away, solves all sorts of scientific problems, not just those of writing. When anthropologists and sociologists do field research, for instance, they typically have problems establishing and maintaining those relationships with people that will let them observe what they want to over a long period of time. Delays and obstructions while you negotiate these arrangements can be discouraging. But experienced fieldworkers know that the difficulties provide valuable clues to the social organization they want to understand. How people respond to a stranger who wants to study them tells something about how they live and are organized. If the poor people in a city neighborhood you want to study are suspicious and won't talk to you, that is a real problem. You may eventually discover that they are standoffish because they think you might be an investigator trying to catch violators of the welfare regulations. The trouble, personally painful, will have taught you something worth knowing.

Similarly, experimental social psychologists got upset when Rosenthal and others demonstrated that an experimenter's seemingly extraneous and irrelevant actions affected the results of experiments independently of the variables supposed to be at work. They shouldn't have. As Rosenthal showed (1966), while psychologists thus lost the illusion of total control over experimental situations, they gained a new and interesting area of study: social influence in small groups. That is gained by talking about the insoluble problem rather than ignoring it.

It's the same with writing. When you can't find the One Right Way to say it, talk about why you can't. Bennett Berger adopted this solution in *The Survival of a Counterculture* (1981), which reported his study of hippie communes in northern California. He was interested in utopian experiments. He felt personally close to the hippie culture and ethos. He wanted to study how communards dealt with the inevitable gap between what they professed and how they behaved as they adapted their beliefs to the circumstances of their lives. He called the methods people used to deal with gaps like that "ideological work" and conceived of studying such work as a microsociology of knowledge. But he had trouble writing about what he found:

> I delayed writing this book for several years because I couldn't find an interpretive frame to put around the social life I observed. Without that frame, I wasn't sure that I understood the meaning of what I was seeing. Without that understanding, I had no posture toward the data, and that reduced my motivation to write. And when that understanding emerged, I didn't like the "cynical" posture it invited me to take.

He described the problem of the cynical posture, which bothered him deeply, as it affected the study he had done in the commune:

> [It is] the tendency of the sociology of knowledge to impugn, weaken, or undermine ideas when analysis of them reveals their self- and group-serving functions. . . . If the idea of urban

apocalypse serves the interests of survival-equipped communards, is that sufficient reason for casting a cold and skeptical eye on it? If the idea of equal rights for children serves the purpose of those adults who initially had neither the time nor the inclination to be middle-class parents, is that sufficient reason for being cynical about their motives? If the affirmation of "authenticity" in interpersonal relationships serves the interests of people so situated that their dense interactional textures make them ill-able to afford emotional disguises, isn't that reason to regard [their belief in] "openness 'n honesty" as simply another self-serving element of ideology (like belief in cultural pluralism by ethnic minorities or in low taxes by the wealthy)? Or on the other hand, when groups are caught in contradictions between the ideas they profess to believe in and their day-to-day behavior, is their hurried ideological repair work best understood in an ironic, contemptuous, and cynical manner?

My answer to these questions is no, at least insofar as the [people he studied] dealt with them. But the answers provided by the major tradition of the sociology of knowledge would seem to be a resounding YES—in part because one of the major motives informing the sociology of knowledge as an intellectual enterprise has been the desire to "unmask" or "demystify" ideas by revealing the "real" interests or functions they serve. (168–69)

"It's easy to see how such a problem can paralyze you: It has taken me a long time to gain the perspective on beliefs and circumstances adopted in this book, and my failure to apprehend it earlier has functioned as a kind of bit in my mouth, preventing me from speaking clearly (223)." Berger wanted to discuss the social bases of what communards believed without making fun of them. Until he could figure out how to do that, he couldn't write his book. I don't want to pursue his argument further (although it deserves to be read in full) because I am citing it as a solution to another kind of problem. Not Berger's problem of how to avoid making fun of what he was studying, but the even more common difficulty of not being able to write because you haven't found the One Right Way to handle that or some other problem. Berger doesn't say how to avoid that fruitless search for the One Right Way, but he demonstrates how. Write about it. Make it the focus of your analysis. He devoted a sizeable part of his book to just that task. In so doing, he found a way to write his book as well as a large subject to embed the story of his research in: the intellectual vice of explanation as a putdown.

Taking readers into your confidence about your troubles requires admitting that you had them and, therefore, that you are not the paragon who always knows the Right Way and executes it flawlessly. I don't think that difficult, since no such paragons exist, but some people don't like to make such admissions. The remedy is to try it and prove to yourself that it doesn't hurt.

Four

Editing by Ear

W hen I edit people's work, or talk about editing to them, they usually want to know (as my friend Rosanna did) what the principles of editing are. What rules do I use to decide, for instance, when to leave a word out or delete a phrase? No one does anything creative by merely following rules (although rules are necessary and helpful), and even the most routine and trivial writing is creative, whether it's a letter to a friend or a note to a delivery person. Unless you are copying a form letter out of a book or writing the fiftieth thank-you note in exactly the words you used for the other forty-nine, you are creating new language, new combinations, something that didn't exist until you put it down that way.

Grammarians and composition teachers recommend several kinds of rules and guidelines. Many rules, like those requiring that a declarative sentence end with a period or that writing proceed from left to right, do what conventions typically do in the arts: make it possible to communicate a thought by providing a minimum of shared understanding between creator and consumer. Other rules make it possible to communicate with less chance of unintended confusion and misunderstanding: rules requiring that pronouns agree with their antecedents, for instance. Still others are not rules at all, but rather guidelines to conventional usage and precise meaning (distinguishing, say, between *reticent* and *reluctant*). Some, finally, are truly matters of taste, about which reasonable people differ, usually along conservative-progressive lines: should I have used the word bullshit in chapter 1?

What role do these rules and guidelines play in the creation of a piece of writing? It might work like this: we put down whatever comes into our heads, then go back over the result with a rulebook in hand, find all the violations of rules, and bring the text into line with the rulebook. Isn't that what we do when we rewrite?

No. We might do something a little like that, but bringing the text into line with the rulebook cannot be so automatic. Bringing it into line is creative too. Furthermore, sociologists' studies of obedience to rules show that rules are never so clear and unambiguous that we can simply follow them. We always have to decide whether a rule exists at all, whether what we have is really covered by the rule, or whether there might not be some exception that isn't in the book but one the rulemakers, we think, must have intended. We also need to interpret rules so that the result we get is reasonable, not some foolishness resulting from blind rule-following. (Harold Garfinkel [1967, 21–4] describes this practice, which he calls ad hocing, as a fundamental feature of all human activity.)

Mike Rose, drawing on his experience in advising students with writer's block, distinguishes two kinds of rules, one clearly better suited to the activity of rewriting:

Algorithms are precise rules that will always result in a specific answer if applied to an appropriate problem. Most mathematical rules, for example, are algorithms. Functions are constant (e.g., *pi*), procedures are routine (squaring the radius), and outcomes are completely predictable. However, few day-to-day situations are mathematically circumscribed enough to warrant the application of algorithms. Most often we function with the aid of fairly general heuristics or "rules of thumb," guidelines that allow varying degrees of flexibility when approaching problems. Rather than operating with algorithmic precision and certainty, we search, critically, through alternatives, using our heuristic as a divining rod—"if a math problem stumps you, try working backwards to solution"; "if the car won't start, check x, y, or z," and so forth. Heuristics won't allow the precision or the certitude afforded by algorithmic operations; heuristics can even be so "loose" as to be vague. But in a world where tasks and problems are rarely mathematically precise, heuristic rules become the most appropriate, the most functional rules available to us. (Rose 1983, 391–2)

Not surprisingly, students who thought rules about writing were algorithms (I'm not inventing straw men—some did) had trouble, while students who used them as heuristics didn't.

We can't, then, write or even rewrite by treating whatever rules we might decide on as algorithms. If not that way, how? We do it by ear. What does that mean? Looking at a blank sheet of paper, or one with writing on it, we use what "sounds good" or "looks good" to us. We use heuristics, some precise, some quite vague.

Most of the time, when social scientists write, they don't think about rules or guidelines at all. Although they don't consult a rulebook, they do consult something: a standard of taste, a generalized notion of what something ought to look or sound like. If the result doesn't conflict too much with that generalized picture they let it stand. They work, in other words, like artists, who

> often find it difficult to verbalize the general principles on which they make their choices, or even to give any reasons at all. They often resort to such noncommunicative statements as "it sounds better that way," "it looked good to me," or "it works."
>
> That inarticulateness frustrates the researcher. But every art's [read "academic discipline's"] practitioners use words whose meanings they cannot define exactly which are nevertheless intelligible to all knowledgeable members of their worlds. Jazz musicians say that something does or does not "swing"; theater people say that a scene "works" or does not "work." In neither case can even the most knowledgeable participant explain to someone not already familiar with the terms' uses what they mean. Yet everyone who uses them understands them and can apply them with great reliability, agreeing about what swings or works, even though they cannot say what they mean.
>
> [This] suggests that they do not work by consulting a set of rules or criteria. Rather, they respond as they imagine others might respond, and construct those imaginings from their repeated experiences of hearing people apply the undefined terms in concrete situations. (Becker 1982a, 199–200)

Sociologists' standards of taste do include rules they learned in composition classes, which they have trained themselves to apply almost automatically. I habitually scan almost anything I read for passive constructions; if it is my prose, I immediately consider whether and how to change them. I am not aware of applying a rule or heuristic and don't consult a book to know when or how to do it. But I know what I am doing and can state the relevant principle if asked (as I did for

Rosanna). Most sociologists use some such rules, many of which unfortunately work as unanalyzed algorithmic stumbling blocks rather than aids.

Most sociologists, however, have few consciously formulated heuristics. More often, they rely on the fallible and uninspected judgments of their ear. They develop that ear, their standards of prose, mainly from what they read. They read work they admire and want what they write to resemble it, to look that way on the page. That probably explains why scholarly writing so often deteriorates as students move through graduate school and into an academic career. They read the professional journals and want their work to look like what they read, for reasons I've already discussed. That suggests an immediate remedy for bad academic writing: read outside your professional field, and when you do, choose good models.

We are not stuck forever with the standard of taste we acquired when we entered our discipline. In fact, we change it considerably, even in the short run. We develop our taste not only from reading, but also from what our friends and peers say to us or what we fear they might say. A colleague of mine feared, when he wrote, the unlikely possibility that his prose would end up at the bottom of a *New Yorker* column as a hideous example of academic writing. Such fears can move a sensitive victim to study a book on style in order to incorporate the heuristics they recommend into his or her standard of taste.

But most sociologists (and probably most academic writers) don't hear many critical remarks about their prose or, if they do, don't hear them from anyone they have to pay attention to. Since ignoring problems of writing causes them no immediate and obvious trouble, they spend their time on statistics and methods and theory, which can and do. Editors and professors reject papers that use statistics incorrectly, but only sigh over those badly written. Because content matters more to a field's progress than style, professors will not flunk smart students who write badly, and some highly esteemed sociologists were notoriously incomprehensible.

The spectacle of a field which cares so little for decent prose may shock outsiders as much it tires insiders, but that is sociology (and probably many other scholarly disciplines), now and in the likely future. As a result, young sociologists have no reason to learn any more about writing than they knew when they began graduate school, and will probably lose some of the skills they do have. If their college English classes have not given them a standard of taste that includes, as working rules, the elements of grammar and style, they will not spend the time to study them seriously. So they will learn to do their editing by ear, if they learn to do it at all.

Since I learned what little I know about writing and editing that way, fortuitously and haphazardly, I find it hard to produce general editorial principles on request. I can, however, give examples, preferably from the work of the person asking the question, and suggest general ideas that seem to be relevant to their problems. Of course, these notions can't be stated algorithmically. I can't say that you must never use passive constructions, but I can say that a particular passive construction misstates an important sociological idea. Nor is it always wrong to use long, abstract words. I have nevertheless, later in this chapter, stated such rules dogmatically because, while passive constructions are sometimes useful, sociologists do not need to be advised to use them, or long, abstract words either. They do those things automatically.

What follow are some examples of how I edit, with some discussion of the choices made, the reasoning behind them, and the guidelines those choices imply. This will put some more flesh on the prescriptions I gave my class. The examples come from early drafts of an article I wrote on photography (Becker 1982b; the published version differs from that quoted here.) The examples are not remarkable; I can find their like in anything I have ever written and in much that I have published.

To begin, consider the following paragraph, which discusses the strategy of describing social groups through photographic portraits of their members:

> Whatever part they [photographers] let stand for the person, the strategy implies a theory and a method. The theory is a simple one, but it is important to make its steps explicit, so that we can see how it works. The theory is that the life a person has lived, its good times and bad, leaves its marks. Someone who has lived a happy life will have a face that shows that. Someone who has managed to maintain their human dignity in the face of trouble will have a face that shows that. . . . This is a daring strategy, because it makes the little that the photograph does contain carry an enormous weight. We must, if the theory is to work and help us to produce effective images, choose faces, details of them, and moments in their history which, recorded on film and printed on paper, allow viewers to infer everything else they are interested in. Viewers, that is, look at the lines on a face and infer from them a life spent in hard work in the sun.

When I began rewriting this passage, the phrase "it is important to," in the second sentence, caught my attention as typical throat clearing. If it's important to do it, don't talk about it, *do it*. (This is a typical guideline which is by no means a rule.) I first changed "it is important to" to "we need to." That made the sentence more active, and slightly stronger, and introduced an *agent*, someone actually doing it. Things that are not done by anyone, but "just are," have a fuzzy quality I don't like.

Having made that change, I still wasn't happy. The sentence had three clauses which were just strung together. If I can rearrange a sentence so that its organization displays and thus reinforces the connections I am describing, I do. So I cut the first clause, putting its content into an adjectival phrase. Instead of saying the theory was a simple one, I replaced "its steps" in the second clause with "the steps of this simple theory." A few words less, and the simplicity of the theory reduced to a small descriptive point: "We need to make the steps of this simple theory explicit. . . ." Having done it, I no longer had to say that we needed to do it, which was no better than saying it was important to do it. The rewritten sentence reads, "If we make the steps of this simple theory explicit, we can see how it works." It has sixteen words instead of twenty-three. The three strung-together clauses now make an if-then argument that is more interesting than the list it replaced.

Now look at the fourth sentence. I changed "Someone" to "People" for no very good reason, mainly because I wanted to get at "managed to maintain." Wordy phrases like "manage to maintain" try to make simple statements sound profound. Talking about people's ability to act evokes the academic urge to profundity. It seems trivial to say that people "can" do something. We prefer to say that they "had the capability of" or "the ability to" or even, striving for simplicity, that they "were able to." I almost invariably use such constructions in early drafts and replace them with "can" when I rewrite. So I changed the sentence to "People who have kept . . ."

Finally, consider the sentence about lines on a face: "Viewers, that is, look at the lines on a face and infer from them a life spent in hard work in the sun." I cut some words that weren't doing much work. I proved that "that is" was meaningless by taking it out and seeing that the sentence lost no meaning. Applying the same test, I changed "a life spent in hard work" to a "life of hard work." But I also saw a way to add a few words and make the image more concrete: "Viewers

look at the lines on a face and infer that they were
baked in during a life of hard work in the sun." A slight
transposition remedies the ambiguity of "they" and
reads even better: "Looking at the lines on a face,
viewers infer that . . ."

The final version, as published, went like this:

> Whatever part a photographer chooses to stand
> for the person, he or she is employing a strategy
> that relies on a theory and a method. This strategy
> depends on the assumption that the experiences
> of life are recorded in faces, that the life a person
> has lived leaves physical marks.
>
> Photographers, accordingly, choose faces, de-
> tails of faces, and moments in their histories
> which, recorded on film and printed on paper,
> allow viewers to deduce what they don't see but
> want to know about. Portraits often contain a
> wealth of detail, so that careful study allows us to
> make complex and subtle readings of the charac-
> ter of the person and of the life-in-society of that
> person. Looking at the lines on a face, viewers
> may conclude that that these were baked in dur-
> ing a life of hard work in the sun. From these same
> lines, they can infer wisdom produced by hard
> work and age or, alternatively, senility and decay.
> To make any of these conclusions, a viewer must
> bring to bear on the image one of several possible
> theories of facial lines.

That doesn't exhaust what might be done here.

Two sentences, farther on in the article, combined
several common difficulties. I gave an example of how
a well-known contemporary photographed the interiors of buildings with people in them: "Some of Robert
Frank's most compelling images are of offices after
hours, with no one there—no one but the janitor
cleaning up. A bank looks different when it is occupied
by a janitor than when it is occupied by bankers."

I might almost leave this, in the style of a mathematics text, as an exercise for the reader to repair. Not to be a tease about it, however, I began by stating the first phrase more actively: "Robert Frank made some of his most compelling images. . . ." That let me rearrange and simplify the next construction: "Robert Frank made some of his most compelling images in offices after hours," and went on, cutting a repetition I thought forceful when I first wrote it, "when no one was there but the janitors." Why did I cut the "cleaning up" that followed "janitors"? Because I now meant to put that thought into a more concrete image in the next sentence, which I changed to: "A bank occupied only by a janitor pushing a mop looks different from one filled with bankers on the phone." That let me contrast the bankers' telephoning and the janitors' mop-pushing, rather than just mentioning their job titles and letting the reader fill in their characteristic actions. The rewritten sentence also eliminates the repetition of something being "occupied by" somebody. Saying that bankers "filled" the space emphasized the contrast between the bustle of daytime business and the quiet of night-time cleaning that Frank's photograph called attention to.

Here are some further short illustrations. I changed "If you do the former [there is no point in explaining the specifics of these examples], you may be able to" to "The former lets you." I changed "Older houses have lots of [if I had said, less colloquially, "many," it wouldn't have made any difference] rooms with doors on them" to "The rooms in older houses have doors on them." (And now, after publication, I realize that I should have deleted "on them" too.) I changed "according to the method just described" to "by the method just described" and "the change that has occurred in conceptions of privacy" to "the change in conceptions of privacy."

We spend a lot of time in my writing seminar making similar changes in specimens donated by friends, colleagues, and eventually the students themselves. Stu-

dents find it difficult at first to understand why, having
rewritten a sentence, I then rewrite it again, and even a
third or fourth time. Why don't I get it right the first
time? I say, and try to show them, that each change
opens the way to other changes, that when you clear
away nonworking words and phrases, you can see more
easily what the sentence is about and can phrase it
more succinctly and accurately.

They also wonder if picking away at such tiny
matters of wording really affects the result. They find
the exercise tedious at first, and to be truthful, I prolong
the first session unforgiveably. I want them to see that
there is always something more to discuss, some further possible change; that I can and probably will
question every word and punctuation mark; and that
they should learn to do likewise. They find the exercise
unnerving. They cannot imagine raising all those questions about every sentence. Eventually I reassure them,
as does their own experience. They discover that the
process doesn't take as much time as they feared, that
you can quickly spot the obvious problems and need
worry only about a few that are truly difficult to solve.
They learn that line by line editing is easy because the
things to fix fall into classes. When you understand the
nature of a class, you know how to fix the problems of
the sentences that belong to it. (This is, I guess, my way
of talking about rules and guidelines.)

What the students accept less easily is that, however
long it takes, such detailed editing is worth doing. They
can see that each change makes things marginally
clearer and cuts out a few words that probably weren't
doing much work anyway. But what good is that? I
know that when I finished *Art Worlds*, I thought I had
done all the editing the prose needed or could stand. A
gifted copy editor, Helen Tartar, went over it and made
hundreds of further changes, few as extensive as the
ones I have just discussed. When I read the material
with her changes, I felt the way I do when, looking
through the viewfinder of my camera, I give the lens

that last quarter turn that brings everything into perfect focus. Good editing does that, and it's worth doing. The unnecessary words take up room and are thus uneconomic. They cheat, demanding attention by hinting at profundities and sophistication they don't contain. Seeming to mean something, those extra words mislead readers about what is being said.

The sentences we just considered exemplify classes of problems and the way the problems can be solved. None of the guidelines I am going to give is original. It would be a wonder if they were. Generations of English teachers, editors, and writers have discovered and rediscovered them, taught them to students, and recommended them to writers. Some word-processing programs even find typical stylistic faults and suggest corrections. Here is my version, tailored to the needs of sociologists, but perhaps useful to scholars in other disciplines as well.

1. *Active/passive.* Every writing text insists that you substitute active verbs for passive ones when you can. (Doesn't that sound better than saying "The necessity of replacing passive verbs with active ones is emphasized in every book on writing"?) What matters more than the grammatical distinction between active and passive is the simple act of putting the crucial actions into verbs and making some important character in the story you are telling the subject of the verb. But paying attention to the grammatical distinction starts you on the right road. Active verbs almost always force you to name the person who did whatever was done (although gifted obfuscators can avoid the requirement). We seldom think that things just happen all by themselves, as passive verbs suggest, because in our daily lives people *do* things and *make them happen.* Sentences that name active agents make our representations of social life more understandable and believable. "The criminal was sentenced" hides the judge who, we know, did the sentencing and, not incidentally, thus makes the criminal's fate seem the operation of impersonal forces rather than the result of people acting together to imprison him or her. Almost every version of social theory insists that we *act* to produce social life. Karl Marx and George Herbert Mead both thought that, but their followers' syntax often betrays that theory.

2. *Fewer words.* Scholarly writers often insert words and whole phrases when they don't want to say something as flatly as it first came to them. They want to indicate a modesty, a reservation, a sense that they know they might be wrong. Sometimes they want to recognize that readers may disagree by suggesting politely, before actually saying whatever they are going to say, that it merits attention, instead of just saying it right out, as though it of course merited attention. That's why I had said at first "it was important" to make the theory's steps explicit. But if it isn't important, why bother to do it? And if it is, won't doing it make that clear enough without a preliminary announcement?

We scholars also use unnecessary words because we think, like the student in my seminar, that if we say it plainly it will sound like something anybody could say rather than the profound statement only a social scientist could make. We give it that special importance by suggesting that some important process underlies what we are talking about. So I had at first spoken of people who "managed to maintain" their dignity. That hints, as "people who have kept" their dignity doesn't, that keeping their dignity was difficult and they had to work at it. But I was writing about photographers, not about people surmounting trouble. While people do *maintain* their dignity, just as the phrase suggests, this article doesn't talk about that, and it was therefore distracting and pointless to mention it. Similarly, "the change *that has occurred* in conceptions of privacy" makes the process of change in those conceptions important. If I delete the italicized words, the point I want to make is intact and I have removed a distracting reference to an unanalyzed process I won't mention again.

Sometimes we put those throat-clearing phrases in because the rhythm or structure of the sentence seems to require it, or because we want to remind ourselves that something is missing in the argument. We want to make an if-then argument, but we haven't consciously worked out the causal connection our intuition thinks is there. So we make the form and hope the content will appear to fill it. Or we do it out of habit. We get attached to locutions and formats. Like many scholarly writers, I often write sentences with three predicate clauses: "This book excites our curiousity, gives us some answers, and convinces us that the author is right." (The second sentence of the next paragraph is another good example, one that occurred naturally as I was writing.) But I often use that form whether I have three things to say or not, and then I have to scratch for the third thing, which is then vacuous. No harm. It comes out in editing.

An unnecessary word does no work. It doesn't further an argument, state an important qualification, or add a compelling detail. (See?) I find unnecessary words by a simple test. As I read through my draft, I check each word and phrase to see what happens if I remove it. If the meaning does not change, I take it out. The deletion often makes me see what I really wanted there, and I put it in. I seldom take unnecessary words out of early drafts. I'll see them when I rewrite and either replace them with working words or cut them.

3. *Repetition.* Scholars create some of their most impenetrable obscurities by trying to be clear. They know that vague pronouns and ambiguous syntax can leave what they mean unclear, so they repeat words and phrases if there is any possibility of confusion. That may not confuse readers, but it usually bores them. I am not simply repeating the mechanical rule we all learned in high school: don't repeat the same word within so-and-so many sentences. You may have to repeat words, but you shouldn't repeat words when you can get the same result without doing it. Remember my sentence: "A bank looks different when it is occupied by a janitor than when it is occupied by bankers." "When it is occupied" doesn't require repetition and makes readers' minds wander. If I think about it, I can create a more compact and interesting sentence, as I tried to do in that example.

4. *Structure/content.* The thoughts conveyed in a sentence usually have a logical structure, stating or implying some sort of connection between the things it discusses. We might want to say that something resembles or actually is something else (state an identity): "A mental hospital is a total institution." We might want to describe an identifying characteristic of a class of phenomena: "People who move from the country are marginal to the urban society they enter." We might want to identify something as a member of a class: "Monet was an Impressionist." We might want to state a causal connection or an if-then relation: "Slums produce crime" or "If a child grows up in a broken home, that child will become delinquent." We can state these connections as I have just done. That will be enough to make our point clear. But we can be even clearer by reinforcing the point syntactically.

Syntax, the way we arrange the sentence's elements, indicates the relations between them. We can reinforce a sentence's thought by arranging its elements so that its syntax *also* makes the argument or, at least, does not interfere with the reader's understanding of it. We can, for example, put subordinate thoughts in subordinate positions in the sentence. If we put them in positions of importance, readers will think they are important. If we make every thought in the sentence equally important grammatically by stringing together coordinate clauses, readers will think they are equally important. That happens when, giving in to habit, I say I have three things to discuss and then label them one, two, and three or just list them one after the other. We can usually make our point more forcefully by going from

one to the next in a way that shows how they are
connected other than by following one another in a list.

5. *Concrete/abstract.* Scholars generally, and sociologists particularly, use far too many abstract words.
Sometimes we use abstractions because we don't have
anything very specific in mind. Scholars have favorite
abstract words which act as placeholders. Meaning
nothing in themselves, they mark a place that needs a
real idea. Complex or complicated and relation exemplify the type. We say that there is a complex relation
between two things. What have we said? "Relation" is
such a general concept that it means almost nothing,
which is why it is so useful in very abstract branches of
mathematics. All it says is that two things are connected somehow. But almost any two things are related
somehow. In disciplines less abstract than mathematics
we usually want to know *how.* That's what's worth
knowing. Complex doesn't tell us, it just says, "Believe
me, there's a lot to it," which most people would
concede about almost anything. Most of the spatial
metaphors used in discussions of social life and other
scholarly topics—levels and positions in social organizations, for instance—cheat readers of concrete specificity that way. So do phrases which hint that what we
are describing is part of a collection of similar things: "a
set of" or "a kind of."

We also use abstractions to indicate the general
application of our thought. We don't want anyone to
think that what we have found out is only true of
Chicago schoolteachers or a mental hospital in Wash-
ington. We want them to understand that what we
found where we did our research can be found under
similar circumstances anywhere in the world, any time
in history. There is nothing wrong with that: it is a
major reason for doing sociological research. We can
best convince readers of the generality of our results by
describing what we have studied in specific detail and
then showing, in similar detail, what class of things it
belongs to and what other things are likely to belong to

that class. If I show in detail how people learn to smoke marihuana from others and how that affects their experience of the drug's effects, I can go on to describe a class of similar phenomena in similar specificity: how people learn from others to understand their inner physical experiences. The specific case I have described in detail provides a model to which readers can refer my more general ideas. Without the specifics, the general ideas don't mean much.

Writing manuals tell us to use concrete details because they make the matter more alive to the reader, more memorable. Williams (1981), for instance, says: "Regardless of our audience, we can make writing readable and memorable by writing specifically and concretely. When we squeeze long, windy phrases into more compact phrases, we make diffuse ideas sharply specific. . . . The more narrow the reference, the more concrete the idea; the more concrete the idea, the clearer and more precise the idea (132–3)."

When we use concrete details to give body to abstractions, however, we should choose the details and examples carefully. The example that readers have in mind will bring in considerations not explicitly addressed in the general argument and color our understanding of it. Kathryn Pyne Addelson, a philosopher who has analyzed the ethical problems of abortion, says that philosophers typically concoct very fanciful examples—of hypothetical women impregnated by flying insects and the like—and that such a choice of examples lets them reach conclusions they would not support if they discussed the case of a pregnant forty-year-old woman with five children whose husband is out of work.

6. *Metaphors.* I am leafing through the current issues of a few journals in sociology (I don't think the results would differ if the journals were in history or psychology or English literature). On almost every page I find trite metaphorical talk. "Some cutting edge seems lacking" in a book being reviewed. Another book "covers a huge terrain." A third deals with "a rich issue that has been impoverished by its context." My colleagues talk about "the growing body of literature," analyses that "penetrate to the heart" of the problem being discussed or "fall between two stools," and find "the seeds" of another society's institutional practices "planted in our own society." A theoretical approach leads to a "conceptual straitjacket." Researchers "mine" data or "ferret" or "tease" results out of them and get to "the bottom line." The most scientific document contains a lot of such metaphorical talk.

I usually cut such metaphors out of anything I am editing. All metaphors? No, only ones like the above. You can see their kind by comparing them to a masterful use of metaphor, Goffman's (1952) well-known paper "On Cooling the Mark Out," which uses the confidence game as a metaphor for those social situations in which someone cannot sustain the definition of self they have offered to themselves and the world. I would leave that metaphor in anything I edited.

The difference between the two kinds of metaphor lies in the seriousness and attention with which they are used. I don't mean how seriously authors take their subject, but how seriously they take the details of their metaphor. Goffman took the con game metaphor seriously. He compared the other situations he analyzed—the lover whose proposal is rejected, the big shot who can't get a table in a crowded restaurant, the person who can't manage the ordinary routines of everyday life well enough to avoid drawing attention to himself—to the con game point for point. In particular, he noted that the marks who lost their money to confidence men realized (and supposed that others would also see) that they were not nearly as smart as they had thought when they tried to get rich quick. Criminal tradition suggested to con men that they could avoid trouble by helping the angry victims restore their self-esteem, by cooling them out. So con men routinely assigned a team member to use well-established methods for achieving that result. Goffman used the metaphor to discover and describe the same job and the same role in restaurants and other places where people were likely to be so exposed, and even suggested that, since some people suffered such exposure in many areas of life, we could probably find professionals who dealt with such problems in a more general way. He identified psychiatry as a discipline devoted to cooling out people whose pretensions social life had unveiled as phony. That discovery validated the metaphor for many readers. But the metaphor validated itself by being serious, by meaning that these other situations were like the con game in all sorts of ways, large and small.

The earlier metaphors I quoted from sociology journals weren't serious about their ramifications. When we say an argument has a "cutting edge," what tool are we comparing it to and what material is it supposed to be cutting? Who "covers terrain" in real life, how do they cover it, and what are the problems of terrain-covering? Is the literature being compared to a human body? Does that mean we should look for its heart, its liver, its stomach, its brain? The authors never meant us to take their metaphors that seriously. The comparisons these "tired metaphors" make no longer live in the minds of those who write them or read them.

A metaphor that works is still alive. Reading it shows you a new aspect of what you are reading about, how that aspect appears in something superficially quite different. Using a metaphor is a serious theoretical exercise in which you assert that two different empirical phenomena belong to the same general class, and general classes always imply a theory. But metaphors work that way only if they are fresh enough to attract attention. If they have been used repeatedly enough to be clichés, you don't see anything new. In fact, you think that they actually mean, literally, what they allude to metaphorically. Take the common expression, "to take the wind out of someone's sails." I had used that, read it, and heard it for years, but it never meant any more to me than that you somehow deflated the person you did it to. Then I learned to sail. In sailing races, your opponents try to come between you and the wind, so that their sail keeps the wind from hitting yours. When they do that successfully, your sails, full of wind and pushing you along briskly a moment before, suddenly begin to flap emptily. The hull's friction in the water, now that no wind is pushing to counteract it, brings the boat to a sudden halt. The metaphor came to life for me, recalling an irritating experience in all its fullness. But the metaphor means little or nothing to people who haven't had that experience.

All the tired metaphors once lived. As metaphors age, they lose their force from sheer repetition, so that they take up space but contribute less than a plain, nonmetaphorical statement. It is clearer and more pointed to say that a book's argument is diffuse than to say that "some cutting edge is lacking." If an author is lucky, no one pays any attention to the literal meaning of the metaphorical statement. When I hear about "babies being thrown out with the bathwater"—and I still do—I find it hard to keep a straight face. The same is true with "falling between two stools." What were those people trying to do with those stools, anyway?

Metaphors also deteriorate from misuse. People who don't know and understand the phenomenon well, who may really not know what they are talking about when they use the words, use them incorrectly, thinking they mean something else. The common metaphor of "the bottom line," for instance, refers to the bottom line of an accountant's report which, summarizing all the previous computations, lets you know whether you made or lost money that year. Metaphorically, it could refer to the final result of any series of calculations: the population of the United States as discovered by the 1980 Census or the correlation between income and education in someone's study. But people often use it to indicate a final offer, the price they will not lower, the indignity they will not suffer: "That's the bottom line! I quit!" People who say that don't know, or don't remember, that the words have a financial referent. They probably use the expression because they like the air of finality "bottom" conveys, implying a point beyond which you can't go.

We can't, and shouldn't try to, avoid using another kind of metaphor, the ones permanently built into our language, which Lakoff and Johnson (1980) have analyzed in great detail. I'll give one example, of what they call

> *orientational metaphors*, since most of them have to do with spatial orientation: up-down, in-out, front-back, on-off, deep-shallow, central-peripheral. These spatial orientations arise from the fact that we have bodies of the sort we have and that they function as they do in our physical environment. Orientational metaphors give a concept a spatial orientation; for example, HAPPY IS UP. The fact that the concept HAPPY is oriented UP leads to English expressions like "I'm feeling up today." (14)

Lakoff and Johnson go on to show how ubiquitously UP and DOWN and their relatives appear in our speech:

> CONSCIOUS IS UP; UNCONSCIOUS IS DOWN
> HEALTH AND LIFE ARE UP;
> SICKNESS AND DEATH ARE DOWN
> HAVING CONTROL or FORCE IS UP;
> BEING SUBJECT TO CONTROL or FORCE IS DOWN
> MORE IS UP; LESS IS DOWN
> FORESEEABLE FUTURE EVENTS ARE UP (AND AHEAD)
> HIGH STATUS IS UP; LOW STATUS IS DOWN
> GOOD IS UP; BAD IS DOWN
> VIRTUE IS UP; DEPRAVITY IS DOWN
> RATIONAL IS UP; EMOTIONAL IS DOWN

Here is their analysis of the last example:

RATIONAL IS UP; EMOTIONAL IS DOWN

> The discussion *fell to the emotional* level, but I *raised* it back *up to the rational* plane. We put our *feelings* aside and had a *high-level intellectual* discussion of the matter. He couldn't *rise above* his *emotions*.

> Physical and cultural basis: In our culture people view themselves as being in control over animals, plants, and their physical environment, and it is their unique ability to reason that places human beings above other animals and gives them this control. CONTROL IS UP thus provides a basis for MAN IS UP and therefore for RATIONAL IS UP. (17)

The book contains over 200 pages of such analyses and examples. As I said, you can't avoid such metaphors. But being aware of them lets you use their overtones purposefully. If you ignore the overtones your prose will fight with itself, the language conveying one idea, the metaphors another, and readers won't be sure what you mean.

This chapter barely touches what goes into creating a standard of taste that will let you edit your own work, and that of others, successfully. The main lesson is not the specifics of what I have said but the Zen lesson of *paying attention.* Writers need to pay close attention to what they have written as they revise, looking at every word as if they meant it to be taken seriously. You can write first drafts quickly and carelessly exactly because you know you will be critical later. When you pay close attention the problems start taking care of themselves.

Five

Learning to Write as a Professional

Sociologists have begun to tell stories on themselves, recognizing that the impersonal reporting of ideas and research results that used to be thought scientific hides facts readers want to know (see the collections of autobiographical pieces edited by Hammond 1964 and Horowitz 1969). Most sociological autobiography has focused on how research is done, and writing deserves the same kind of attention.

I have already discussed how the institutions of scholarly life, especially schools, create the problems of scholarly writing. That discussion focused largely on the earliest phases of the scholarly career: school and just beyond. This chapter and the next look at writing problems as they arise at later stages of a career in sociology. In chapter 6, Pamela Richards discusses the crucial transition from the early post-student days to being a grown-up professional. This most immodest chapter in an immodest book tells some stories from my

thirty-plus years in the business and draws some analytic points from them.

The chief point is that no one learns to write all at
once, that learning, on the contrary, goes on for a
professional lifetime and comes from a variety of experiences academia makes available.

Sociologists don't think of writing as a serious problem until they have trouble getting their work written
or published. They may dismiss it as blithely as an
acquaintance who said, "Writing style? You mean
when to underline and put in footnotes?" They may
treat the skill of writing as a gift of God which they just
happen not to have received, like the student who
explained to his thesis committee (I was a member) that
he knew his thesis was badly written but, you see, he
wasn't verbal. They may realize that they have difficulty saying what they mean, but they think that they
can farm the job out. The nonverbal student said it was
OK because his wife was an English major and could
take care of any problems. Others settle for hiring an
editor they can ill-afford.

Not everyone develops the sensitivity that I did
about writing clearly. I can pinpoint some of the events
of academic life (largely lucky accidents I was, for
whatever reason, ready to respond to) that sensitized
me. English courses had something to do with it. As an
undergraduate at the University of Chicago, I had a
good practical course in writing, which concentrated
on techniques of organization and rewriting. I probably
learned there that the first draft was just a first draft that
I should routinely expect to rewrite. On the other hand,
a few years of graduate school, reading sociology books
and journals, gave my style all the typical features I
now edit out of my own students' work.

After I got my degree, several experiences with
people who were now academic colleagues rather than
teachers reminded me of that undergraduate wisdom. I
got a Ph.D. in sociology from the University of Chicago
in 1951, at the age of twenty-three. Not surprisingly, I

had trouble finding an academic job. Why should anyone hire such a child when they could have a full-grown adult for the same price (at that time, four thousand dollars a year)? I was lucky to get a research job, studying marijuana use, at seventy-five dollars a week. During the Christmas vacation, a Chicago street-car fell over onto an automobile driven by a member of the teaching staff of the Social Science II course at the University of Chicago. They needed a replacement in a hurry, and some friends already teaching the course knew me and vouched for me, so I got the job. That was how I met Mark Benney (since deceased), a British journalist who had begun adult life as a petty criminal and ended up teaching social science through the encouragement and help of David Riesman and Everett Hughes. He had published several books, and his experience as a professional writer showed in the grace and clarity of his prose, which I admired. Small, thin, and prematurely bald, Mark had a devious way that I attributed to his prison stretches. He was careful about what he said, so if he said something serious, you knew he meant it, and meant you to take it seriously.

I had already published an article or two in professional journals and must have thought I was pretty good, or at least competent. I drafted a paper based on my thesis, the study of Chicago public school teachers I've already mentioned. It raised some problems about education and social class that I thought would interest Mark, so I asked him to read it. When he gave it back, he said it was very interesting and then raised some points about the substance. Seemingly as an afterthought, he added, "Of course, I suppose you have to write it in that funny style to get it published in a sociological journal." I knew that he was a "real writer," so the remark stung, and I determined to go back and do it again, using some of the lessons about rewriting I had learned in college. I began to see that finishing a paper didn't mean you were done with it.

Several years later Jim Carper and I wrote an article

based on our study of the occupational identities of graduate students in several fields. We submitted it to the *American Journal of Sociology*, then edited by Everett Hughes, who had directed my thesis research and to whom I felt close and loyal. The manuscript came back, with a note from the managing editor, Helen McGill Hughes (Everett's wife and a sociologist as well as a journalist), saying that I was to understand that Everett really loved me, that he had written his editorial comments at four in the morning, and that I shouldn't take their violence literally. The comments certainly took me aback. Among other things, he said that whole sentences and paragraphs sounded like they had been translated from German, word for word. I didn't read German (or any other language, despite passing a university exam in French to qualify for the Ph. D.), but I knew that was bad. One memorable paragraph quoted one of our most ponderous sentences and added this commentary (given here in its entirety): "Stink! Stink! Stink!" Mark's casual joke had sensitized me. Everett's letter strengthened my desire to write clear, understandable prose that sounded like it had been English all along.

The final step in my addiction to serious rewriting came when Blanche Geer joined Hughes and me in a study of medical students. She took writing very seriously and taught me about it through serious discussions over single words in the drafts we were doing. We had wonderful and interminable discussions, for instance, about "perspective," a word and idea central to the theoretical apparatus of our study. The question was what verb we should use with it. Did people "hold" a perspective, or "have" one? Maybe they "used" a perspective. Each word's overtones were different, and distinguishable, once we focused on them. So the question was not which word was right, but what we wanted to say. We discovered problems through stylistic discussion, but we finally had to solve them theoretically.

Our conversations taught me that it really mattered how you said things and that you had a choice in the matter. They also taught me that rewriting was fun, a kind of word puzzle whose point was to find a really good economical way to say something clearly. My talks with Geer completed my conversion to taking writing seriously and were by far the most important of all these experiences, because they continued through our writing of a number of papers and books together.

The sociologists I had gone through graduate school with had habitually traded drafts of papers-in-progress with each other, and we had been pretty good about telling each other what needed doing next. I don't think I realized how this reading and commenting and being read and commented on among peers affected my professional development until I hired Lee Weiner as a research assistant a few years after I started teaching at Northwestern. I was away the summer he began work, and as a conscientious revolutionary, Lee (who later became one of the Chicago Seven) read all my correspondence, although it was not part of his duties. When I returned in the fall, he told me excitedly how much he had learned by looking through the folders I kept on papers I had written, seeing what my friends had written on, and about, succeeding drafts, and how I had taken those comments into account in my next version.

Several years out of graduate school then, I had built a pretty efficient writing routine around rewriting on the basis of friendly criticism of early drafts. I had learned to see rewriting as fun, something like doing crossword puzzles, not as an embarassing task whose necessity revealed my shortcomings. I learned that thinking about writing, experimenting with my own style, and tinkering with other's work were fun too.

Maybe thinking of writing as an enjoyable game immunized me against the anxieties other people describe, but my relative lack of writing anxiety also had sociological roots. I had grown up in a strong theoretical tradition which also had a strong organizational base. The Chicago school of sociology developed at the University of Chicago in the 1920s, under the leadership of Robert E. Park. (See, for further discussion of the Chicago school, Faris 1967, Carey 1975, and Bulmer 1984.) It had a coherent point of view, embodied in Park's writings and developed and carried on by a cohort of powerful thinkers and doers, most prominently Everett C. Hughes, Herbert Blumer, Louis Wirth, and Robert Redfield. It also had a long list of classic empirical monographs to its credit: *The Gold Coast and the Slum, The Taxi Dance Hall, The Gang* and, later, *French Canada in Transition* and others. I studied, along with a couple of hundred other post–World War II students, with the giants of the post-Park generation and grew up on that pile of monographs. We knew there were other ways of doing sociology, but few of us took them very seriously. Growing up in that tradition and setting gave me a theoretical arrogance, the comforting conviction that I had essentially learned all the general theory I would ever need to know from Hughes and Blumer, and that the theory was good enough to deal with any problem that came up. I knew, and know, better intellectually, but that hasn't affected the emotional result.

Knowing you are essentially right takes a lot of pressure off your writing, since you don't then try to solve sociological problems by finding the just-right way to formulate them. Some people solve theoretical problems by logical analysis. I learned to decide theoretical problems empirically. Either way is better than trying to do it by finding the right way to say it.

The growing number of sociologists and sociological specialties has produced a similar increase in sociological organizations and journals. Sociologists edit these journals, and editorial jobs are usually one of the honors that come to people who have been in the business for a while. Graduate training programs do not teach you how to edit a journal—how to copy edit papers, how to deal with the printer, or how to coax authors to improve their work. Most journals cannot afford professional editors, so the sociologists who become editors do all that themselves. They learn the job by doing it, with the help of a few tips from their predecessors. My experiences as an editor, during which a hobby became a second profession, contributed a lot to my views on writing.

After years of editing the works of friends and colleagues informally, I took on two serious editorial jobs. In 1961 I became editor of *Social Problems*, the official journal of the Society for the Study of Social Problems, an organization that had been started in opposition to the monolith the American Sociological Association was turning into. I understood my job to be (and I think it was so understood by those members of the SSSP who had an opinion) to put out a journal that was somehow different from the "establishment" *American Sociological Review* and *American Journal of Sociology*. I wasn't sure what that entailed, but I thought I ought to try to find a home for articles that were not welcome, for one or another reason, in the larger journals.

What would make an article unwelcome? Most SSSP members thought that the establishment favored heavily quantitative work, work based on structural-functional theory, and work that was apolitical (and therefore in a real sense conservative). The SSSP thus favored work that was nonconservative, not biased toward the quantitative, and used either "Chicago" or, in later years, Marxist theories. In any event, it wanted to be open to whatever wasn't Eastern establishment. I must have accepted all that as reasonable, even though establishment journals had published my own nonquantitative, non-structural-functional work often enough.

So I took over as editor with the notion that my responsibilities consisted of publishing antiestablishment materials. I had also decided (though no one made this part of my official or unofficial responsibili-

ties) that I was going to do something about what I
thought was the sad state of sociological writing by
rewriting what appeared in the journal as much as
necessary. With that in mind, I recruited people for my
editorial board who wrote well and knew what good
writing was and who I could therefore count on to help
me.

I learned a lot from my first few issues. Once I
assembled my first issue (and I'll speak about those
problems shortly), I rewrote every paper in it extensively. That was a more intensive and more educational
experience of editing than I had ever had. Doing so
many papers by so many people in so many styles in
such a short time made me feel like a newspaper copy
editor. I learned to go through a paper rapidly and to
spot the things I knew I would without doubt change
immediately. (I never understood how I did some of
what I learned to do: for instance, to spot a typograph-
ical error in a page of galley proofs from across the room
when I couldn't even read the type.) But I also learned
that I was not going to rewrite all the papers that way,
much as they might need it. It took too long, and I had
other things to do. I might do a few pages of a piece, to
show authors what I had in mind, but after that they
would have to do it themselves or it wouldn't get done.
In the last few years, some larger journals have begun to
employ copy editors, but even they cannot afford what
it would cost to edit journal articles the way, say, a
textbook is rewritten.

I learned another lesson when I assembled the articles for my first issue. A journal is supposed to come
out regularly, every second month, like the *AJS* or *ASR*,
or quarterly, like *Social Problems*. If you missed your
deadline, you lost your turn in the printer's queue,
people complained about their magazine being late,
and the officers of the sponsoring organization wanted
to know what was wrong. Better to come out on time.
That did not mean that you published work you didn't
think was good, but that you published work that was

good, no matter what its breed: quantitative or qualitative, Chicago-style or structural-functional. Every journal editor I have ever talked to has agreed that, whatever prejudices they secretly expected to implement on assuming office, they soon found that the main thing was to get enough decent articles to fill the journal and get it out on time. Authors who think editorial prejudice accounts for their work being turned down or sent back to "revise and resubmit" are, for that reason, almost always wrong.

Of course, a lot of prejudice can be hidden in the definition of a "decent article." But here I am convinced by Stinchcombe (1978), who argues that when sociological analysts are doing good work they are all doing the same thing. Their work often looks more different than it is because they try to inflate its significance by using "portentous names," derived from "epochal theories" to describe what they do. (Many fields in the social sciences and humanities foster this practice, not just sociology.) Because good work is basically the same whatever its theoretical label, "good" is a professional and catholic judgment, like the judgments of musicians or dancers, who usually recognize when others are performing well, even if the judge doesn't care much for what they are doing. When sociologists show me work they think has been turned down because of prejudice, it is almost always badly organized and badly written. (I know that that is the voice of the establishment talking and don't know how to convince skeptics I am right, other than to point to the contents of the journals, which are always more various than critics think.) The prejudices that do exist operate more subtly, as when the editor decides that one badly written, poorly organized piece is worth putting some special effort into, but not another. The lesson for people who do unpopular work is not that they can't get published but that they shouldn't expect editors to do their work for them. No one should, but some have a better chance of that happening.

I had a different editorial experience when I undertook to edit a series of books for the Aldine Publishing Company in 1962. Alexander Morin, then president and himself a social scientist, thought it would be worthwhile to put together a series that represented the Chicago tradition, broadly conceived. This led me to deal with book-length manuscripts and with authors who had the anxiety that goes with the commitment to a book. I also learned the necessity of thinking about how much a book could be expected to sell, not because Morin was a crass businessman but because if too many books lost money there wouldn't be any series. I learned the importance of subject matter and having something to say about it. People who did not care about your fabulous contribution to social theory might nevertheless read your book because they cared about the problems of death in hospital settings or the way mental illness was defined by family members, professionals, and the courts. We eventually published some fifteen books, and the series was reasonably successful, the sellers making up for the bad guesses.

Working as a book editor showed me a larger dimension of editing. I found that I could see an inner logic struggling to express itself in others' work more easily than I could see it in my own, just as I could see redundancy, fancy talk, and all the other faults in their prose more easily than in my mine. Since I wanted to criticize manuscripts in a way that would induce authors to fix them rather than just get mad (otherwise there would be no books for the series), I had to learn to be precise about what bothered me. I also had to tell them the facts of life about commercial publishing. I explained to first authors who had taken their contract to a lawyer that, yes, the contract did favor the publisher but not to worry about it since few publishers took advantage of those clauses. (With more and more publishers becoming subsidiaries of conglomerates, that advice may not be as true as it used to be.)

My own experience with editorial prejudices has

been minimal. The one area where I suffered a little had to do with a major change in the practice of sociology journal editors. My first articles, drawn from my master's thesis, were about jazz musicians. Following the practice of the exemplars I had used (e.g., Oswald Hall's articles on medical careers and Whyte's *Street Corner Society*), I quoted extensively from my field notes and interviews. But musicians didn't talk as politely as doctors (or as Hall reported they talked). They said "shit" and "fuck" a lot and, in the interest of scientific accuracy, and with a little mischief in my heart, I quoted them verbatim. That was acceptable in my thesis but editors in the fifties routinely replaced these words with dashes: "f——" and "s——." (This practice reached a height of foolishness in a postwar issue of the *AJS* devoted to the U.S. Army, in which Fred Elkin's article "The Soldier's Language" ended up largely dashes.) I forget which of my articles was finally allowed to contain bad words written out; it might only have been when they were published in *Outsiders* in 1963. Of course, dirty talk now appears routinely in published sociology.

When I described my writing seminar in chapter 1, I said that I had told the class about my own writing rituals, but I didn't say what they were. Since I began giving the class, I have started writing on a computer, so that I no longer do what I described there. But here is what I told the class then; it's the way I wrote most of what I have written, and I am not sufficiently aware of my new computerized routine to give a fair account. (What I can say of it is to be found in chapter 9.) The entire procedure is tailored to the rhythms of the academic year.

I am lazy, don't like working, and minimize the time I spend at it. So, although I have written a fair amount, I have spent relatively little time at the typewriter. I would begin what eventually became a paper by talking, to anyone who would listen, about the topic I was going to write about. When I began teaching, that meant

that I talked to my classes about it. (Art Worlds started
out as the transcribed recordings of the lectures I gave
the first time I taught the sociology of art, eight or nine
years before the book was finished.) If I was invited to
give a talk somewhere, I tried to persuade people that
they wanted to hear about my "new research interest,"
that is, the paper I was beginning to work on. Those
talks did some of the work of a rough draft. I learned
what points I could get to follow one another logically,
which ways of making a point people understood, and
which ways caused confusion, what arguments were
dead ends that were better not entered at all.

I had not, when I began relying on talking as a way of
getting something started, read David Antin's explanation of why he writes by talking, but I recognized my
own feelings in his description:

> because ive never liked the idea of going into a
> closet to address myself over a typewriter   what kind
> of talking is that?   ive gotten into the habit of going
> to some particular place   with something on my mind
> but no particular words in my mouth   looking
> for a particular occasion to talk to particular people in a
> way i hope is valuable for all of us
>
> (Antin, 1976, i)

After talking about something for a while (usually
several months or longer) I would get restless. I seldom
recognized the feeling for what it was. It ordinarily did
not strike me during the school year or even during
most of the summer vacation. We have for many years
spent our summers, and any other time off from teaching, in San Francisco, returning to Chicago just in time
for the beginning of the fall quarter. About three weeks
before the day we departed, I would suddenly, with no
premonitory symptoms I could notice other than this
vague restlesness, sit down and start typing all day and
half the night. I typed double-spaced on legal-size
yellow ruled pads. I tore each sheet off the pad carefully. If it didn't tear neatly at the perforations, I didn't

use it. I didn't rewrite—not then, anyway—just kept typing. If I had trouble making a point or couldn't see how to end an argument, I made brackets by combining the slash and the underline (I love the computer's ability to produce several varieties of brackets) and said something like "I can't get anywhere with this now." Then I went on to some other point I could write about.

I added up my production frequently and announced to anyone who would listen that I had done six pages or, counting lines and estimating words to a line, 2500 words. I tried to avoid crossing anything out, but was not rigid about it. If I saw a better way to say something, I replaced the old phrasing with something better. I also, quite neatly, inserted new passages where I thought them necessary, either by cutting and pasting or marking in the text on page 7 where the inserted material on my new page 7A would go. (It pleased me when secretaries complimented my neat manuscripts.) I have written as many as three ten-to-fifteen page manuscripts—rough drafts of articles—in a three week period.

So I would return from California with these rough drafts and spend the school year tinkering with them. I often put them away for several months and seldom thought of them as the routine of teaching—attending meetings, talking with students and colleagues—took over my daily life. That helped me redo the papers because, during the interim, I would forget why a particular point or way of expressing it was so necessary and find it easier to change them. I might not take any of these folders out and begin rewriting until the Christmas vacation. I always began by fixing sentences: cutting excess words, clarifying ambiguities, amplifying telegraphic thoughts. As I told my class, doing that invariably brought up the theoretical difficulties I had papered over, so that I soon had to reconsider my whole analysis. When I could, I wrote a new version of the parts that didn't work. If I couldn't, I didn't. In either case, I usually put the paper away again, for months or sometimes years.

From here on, the description fits my new computerized habits as well, and I will speak in the present tense. Eventually I make another draft. I can do this kind of work any time and usually spend no more than a few hours a day for three or four days at it. After a second or third draft, I have something I can send to some friends who might have helpful thoughts or harsh criticisms. I prefer hearing those criticisms in private from my friends rather than publicly in a "Letter to the Editor."

Some papers never get finished, but I hate to waste anything I write and never give up hope, not even on pieces no one likes. I have had some things in my files for twenty years (in fact, I am still nursing an even older paper on the Abbey Theatre that I wrote for Everett Hughes's class in ethnic relations in 1948).

When I get criticisms and comments, from friends or from editors who have rejected a paper, I assume that I have failed to make my points clearly enough to forestall the objections they make, and look for what I can do to meet the objections without changing my position, unless the criticism convinces me that the position requires changing. This revising and rethinking goes on until I can't think of anything else to do with it, or until some home for the piece presents itself (that is, until I am asked to prepare something for some occasion or volume, and what I have been working on fits the specifications). I have sometimes thought I was done with a piece of writing and then discovered that I wasn't. How do I know that? When I see something that can be done better than it is, and see a way to do it, I know that I will have to go through the manuscript one more time. (I twice thought *Art Worlds* was finished before it really was.)

As I accumulated experience and became more cocksure, I began to set myself writing problems. Becoming dissatisfied with the long, complicated sentences I was writing, I started experimenting with short ones. How few words could I use? Very few. I also began searching for alternatives to the third person (too pompous) and the first person (tiresome in excess and often inappropriate). That led to an orgy of second persons, stage whispers to the reader: "You can see how this would lead to . . ."

Such a routine presupposes that the writer can afford to wait as long as I habitually do to finish things. When you write to a deadline—if, say, you have agreed to contribute a chapter to a book, and the deadline is approaching, or you have agreed to give a paper at the annual meeting of the American Sociological Association—you don't have that luxury. You don't have it, either, if you need publications to convince your colleagues or some administrator that you deserve promotion. One way around the latter problem is to do something that necessity forced on me early in my professional life. Because I had research, rather than teaching, jobs for many years, I always had to start new projects before I had finished old ones. As a result, I was always working on several generations of writing simultaneously: roughing out an initial draft of something new, rewriting initial drafts from an older project, making the final revisions in something ready for press. That is easier than it sounds. In fact, it makes every step of the process easier because when you get stuck on one job you can turn to another, always doing what comes easiest.

When I started making photographs in 1970, the standard photographic practices I then learned gave me more ideas about writing. I learned, as all photo students do, that the most important thing a photographer can do is photograph and that making thousands of bad photographs is no disgrace as long as you make a few good ones too and can tell the good from the bad. Students learn to "read" a contact sheet, made by printing a cut-up roll of film on one sheet of paper, so that each frame is reproduced at its actual size. You see every exposure you made, and you learn how to tell which one has an idea worth pursuing. It's the perfect way to learn that all that counts is the final product and that no one will criticize you for false starts and wrong ideas if you find something good in the process. I learned to be prodigal with film, paper, and my time. That carried over to my writing. I became more willing than ever to write down any damn thing that came into my head, knowing by analogy with photographing that I could always weed out what I didn't like or couldn't use.

Sometime in the seventies, I began to develop literary pretensions and ambitions. I think this started when a friend who was a "real writer" (a writer, that is, of fiction) said kind things about some drafts of an essay I was writing on art worlds. I began to wonder if I couldn't make the writing better in a more extended sense than just clarity. I began experimenting with a kind of organization I had barely been aware of before. I began to plant the seeds of ideas to be explored later in the early sections, and to introduce examples that I would later use to recall a complex point for readers. I quoted Anthony Trollope's story (from his autobiography) about relying on an old manservant to bring him coffee before he began writing and his comment that he thought that servant deserved as much credit as Trollope himself for the resulting books. I let that stand for the artist's dependence on the help of others for getting the work done, and later in the book I just referred to Trollope and his servant, expecting readers to recall the theoretical point.

Perhaps as a result of my experiences in teaching, I have become more and more convinced of the importance of stories—good examples—in the presentation of ideas. I used to be irritated when students told me that what they remembered from my sociology of art course was the story of Simon Rodia and the Watts Towers, which I told in enormous detail and illustrated with slides. I wanted them to remember the theories I was so slowly and painfully developing. Later I decided that the stories were more important than the theories. In a way, I should have known that, because I always began writing reports of field research by picking out representative incidents and quotes from my field notes and arranging them in some order, then writing a commentary on them.

Art Worlds also introduced me to the problems and opportunities of illustrations. It was obvious that a book on the arts should be illustrated. I first experimented with that possibility in a mischievous way. The *American Journal of Sociology* had accepted, after many revisions, an article called "Arts and Crafts," which dealt with the way some craft media got taken up by worlds of art. In the course of the paper, I described a number of art works that illustrated my analytic points. When the article was accepted, I called the managing editor and asked if she didn't think that some illustrations would be appropriate. The *AJS* almost never published pictures, other than portraits of deceased members of the University of Chicago Sociology Department, and I think I assumed that she would say no, and I could then feel discriminated against. Naturally, she said that she would ask the printer and the editor, but thought they would say yes, as they did. Now I had more work to do, finding pictures that really made the points I wanted to make and for which I could get prints at a reasonable cost. The text had referred to Robert Arneson's ceramic sculpture of a teapot whose spout was an erect penis, and to a photograph of a nude woman by Edward Weston. I thought that perhaps there would be trouble over these (the Weston photograph included pubic hair, which had only recently made *Playboy*) but my prejudices were wrong again.

When I put the book together, I knew that it would have pictures. Grant Barnes, my editor at the University of California Press, gave me a wonderful piece of advice. He said, "Don't put captions on the pictures that just identify them. Say at least a sentence explaining what the reader should see in the picture." Since I followed that advice, a reader can get the gist of the book just by looking at the pictures and reading the captions. All this has increased my interest in the visual aspects of writing and bookmaking. I expect my new computer's ability to produce pictures and unusual typefaces to be a help with that.

To repeat the moral, the only good reason for talking so much about myself, you learn to write from the world around you, both from what it forces on you and from what it makes available. The institutions scholars work in push them in some directions, but also open up a lot of possibilities. That's where you make a difference. I have been relatively open to the possibilities, perhaps more than most, and resistant (again, perhaps more than most) to the pushes. The world does push and sometimes it hurts to resist. But my story, I think, for all its historical and personal peculiarities, shows that the opposite is truer than most people think.

Six

Risk

by Pamela Richards

The bulk of this chapter is by Pamela Richards, a sociologist who teaches at the University of Florida, but it needs some introduction and explanation. I had been very pleased with the results of asking Rosanna Hertz to write to me about what she meant when she said that some ways of writing were "classy." I was therefore on the lookout for a chance to see what else I could discover by persuading people to write to me about what they meant by their offhand remarks. I didn't have long to wait.

I have known Pamela Richards since she began her graduate work at Northwestern. After graduating and beginning her teaching career at Florida, she continued to do technical statistical studies in criminology, in the style of her dissertation. After several years, she decided to try something different and use her substantial fieldwork skills to do a study of the Florida state women's prison located near Gainesville. She thought

the study would be more difficult than it turned out to
be. The prison officials made her entrance easy, and
the residents, initially suspicious, soon talked to her
freely and gave her access to most prison activities.

After a year she had accumulated a substantial file
of field notes and knew a great deal about life in this
prison. She thought she ought to begin writing up her
results. We had corresponded earlier about her fieldwork problems, so she confided that she was having
trouble getting started. Since she had successfully
written up her earlier research, she thought there might
be something about qualitative materials that required
a different approach, and she asked me about it.

I brought out my standard remedy, mentioned earlier, suggesting that she sit down and write whatever
came into her head, as though the study were done, but
without consulting her field notes, the literature on
prisons, or anything else. I told her to keep typing as
fast as she could. When she got stuck, I suggested, she
should type in "I'm stuck" and go on to another topic.
Then she could read the results and see what she
thought was true. In that way, she would find out how
to analyze her field materials, because she would have
to check them to see if what she thought was true really
was and, if not, what was. In any case, I said, she could
produce a lot of rough draft quickly, and that would be
a start.

I have given this advice to many people over the
years. Not many take it. They don't argue with me, they
just don't do it. I had always found that hard to
understand, but the results of my advice to Pamela
helped me to see why they were so balky. She wasn't
balky, but, because she was reflective and articulate,
she could make clear what others had found troublesome.

For a while, I heard nothing from her. Then she
wrote to say that she had followed my advice and was
enclosing the fifty pages she had written in ten days as
a result. That tickled me, of course. It's rewarding to see

your advice pay off. But her accompanying letter raised what turned out to be an important question, one for which, with a little prodding, she provided a wonderfully detailed answer.

She wrote that she had rented a cabin in the woods to live in while she tried the experiment of writing the draft. "Even though I knew it would be a very high-risk operation," she said, "I decided to try it anyway." I couldn't understand what she meant. She was a well-established professional who had published in respected journals and coauthored a book. She gave papers at professional meetings and had just been promoted and given tenure. She had, in other words, been through the scariest trials that afflict young academics. Where was the risk?

Here was my chance to use the "research method" that had been so successful with Rosanna Hertz. I wrote Pamela, asking her to explain what was so risky about sitting at a typewriter for ten days and writing any damn thing that came into her head. At worst, I pointed out, she would have wasted the time she had spent on it, but that can never be much of a price for someone who otherwise might not have written anything at all.

Again I didn't hear for a while. Then I got the letter that follows, explaining honestly and personally what lay behind that casual remark. I originally intended to use what she wrote as raw material for an analysis of the problems of risk. As I reread what she had written, however, it was clear that I could add very little to her story and analysis. So I asked her if she would be author of the body of this chapter, for which I would simply write an introduction and whatever else was necessary to relate it to the rest of the book. She agreed. It's an unorthodox way of doing things, but it seems the best and most honest way of getting what needs to be said said. What follows is her letter answering my question.

Dear Howie,

I just finished two cups of coffee while thinking about the issue of risk. My meditations have to start with three dreams that I've had in the last week. Two are about risk (among many other things, I'm sure) and one is about pushing through the risk. Actually, only two are dreams, the other is a different sort of midnight event that I suffered through right before I received your letter.

In my first dream, I had sent copies of three chapter drafts to a close friend I've known since graduate school. They were the same drafts that I'd sent to you. (I haven't really sent her anything yet.) She and I met at the American Sociological Association meetings in San Francisco, and she brought a huge stack of written comments with her. She was *angry* with me, and the comments were scathing. They went on for page after page: "This is absolutely the stupidest stuff you've ever written. . . . How could you say such things?. . . . Don't you realize the politically objectionable nature of what you've said here. . . . What's wrong with you, haven't you any sense at all? . . . This is nothing but bullshit. . . ." As I read through the stack of comments, she sat there and simply glowered at me, and I felt like she wanted to take me by the shoulders and shake me till my teeth fell out. Naturally I began to cry—silently, with the tears running down my face. I wanted to wail and keen and run away, but because we were at the meetings and there were all these *colleagues* around, I had to keep as good a face on it as possible. I felt terrible. Betrayed, perhaps, but mostly as if I had let her down. I felt that I had failed to measure up to what she expected of me, and that this preliminary work had somehow demonstrated that I was a shit—intellectually, personally, politically, and morally. I struggled up from the table where I was reading the comments. She leaned back in her chair and watched me. Her face was cold and the anger had turned to disgust. Then somehow I was pushing my way through a crowd of

conventioning sociologists (none of whom I knew),
trying to get out. I kept bumping into them, saying
"Excuse me," but no one responded much. They didn't
even really look in my direction when I ran right into
them. Then I woke up.

Now for some balance. I had a second dream that
night, it seemed to be right after that one. (I'd been
reading Lillian Hellman's *An Unfinished Woman* and
Pentimento. Over and over and over. I don't quite know
why.) In the second dream I was sitting in a chair
composing things for the book on the women's prison.
I'm not sure what chapter or what topic, but the words
were flowing beautifully. I wasn't writing them down;
instead I was speaking them, and they just rolled out of
my mouth. Everything was perfect, the style was gor-
geous, and I was conscious of the fact that it all
sounded as if Lillian Hellman were writing it—it was
exactly the same style, the same marching sentences,
the same feel and expression. It was wonderful. I felt
very powerful and fully in command of what I was
doing. I knew it was good stuff, knew it was elegant,
and even began gesturing as I was speaking, almost as if
it were oral interpretation. When I awoke, I just sort of
floated up into consciousness slowly and comfortably,
very pleased with myself and what I had accomplished.

But then, two nights ago I flashed out of a deep sleep
(no dream this time) with a perfectly formed, crystal-
line conviction. I *knew*, absolutely and with complete
certainty, that I was a fraud. The knowledge wasn't
constructed through some explicit argument; it didn't
develop out of anything I recognized; it was just *there*.
So I began turning it over in my mind, trying to see
what might be on the underside, and it began to take on
better form: "I am a fraud because I don't work the way
everyone else does. I don't read the classics as bedtime
reading; hell, I don't read anything except weird novels
and stuff that has nothing to do with my 'work.' I don't
sit in the library taking notes; I don't read the journals
cover to cover; and what's worse, I don't want to. I am

not a scholar. I am not a sociologist because I don't
know any sociology. I haven't the commitment to steep
myself in the ideas and thoughts of The Masters. I
couldn't converse meaningfully about The Literature
on any topic including those in which I am allegedly a
specialist. Even worse, I have the temerity to claim that
I am doing a study of women's prisons, when in fact I
haven't done it right. I don't know all sorts of things I
ought to know, and can't seem to force myself to do it
the way it ought to be done. Worse still, I know I have
to go back soon and do another data push, filling in the
holes, expanding things, and doing it right this time.
And I don't want to. I'm too tired."

Not too useful for the middle of the night, right? God,
it was torture. I went round and round on these sorts of
things, getting angry and frightened by turns. I simply
couldn't shake the conviction that I was a fraud. The
main reason? I don't "do sociology" the way all my
colleagues appear to do it, and the way it's supposed to
be done. (And I've had a dry period as far as writing
goes—almost two weeks—which leads rapidly to the
conviction that I am a lazy parasite who doesn't do
anything, anything at all.) The fact that I *know* that no
one works the way they say they do, and that no one
hews the perfect methodological line doesn't help
much because I cannot translate this knowledge into
gut-level belief. I feel vulnerable. Others can get me if I
let on that I am a misshapen lump of a sociologist, even
if they are equally misshapen.

So what does all this have to do with risk? For me,
sitting down to write is risky because it means that I
have to open myself to scrutiny. To do that requires that
I trust myself, and it also means that I have to trust my
colleagues. By far the more critical of these is the latter,
because it is colleagues' responses that make it possible
for me to trust myself. So I have dreams of self-doubt
and personal attack by one of my closest and most
trusted friends.

God, it's hard to trust colleagues. There's more at

stake than simply being laughed at. Every piece of work can be used as evidence about what kind of a sociologist (and person) you are. Peers read your work and say, "Hell, that's not so bright. I could do better than that. She's not so hot after all." (And, by extension, they decide that your public act of sociologist is fraudulent.) The discipline is set up in such a competitive fashion that we assuage our own insecurities by denigrating others, often publicly. There's always a nagging fear (for those of us who are junior, unknown sociologists) that even peers can make offhand comments about us that will become part of our professional image. If those comments are critical or negative, it's dangerous. This makes it very risky to give drafts of anything to peers. Few people understand what working drafts are. They assume that first drafts are just one step removed from being sent out for review. So if you show up with a working first draft, you worry about what could happen. They could decide that it's shoddy work, poorly constructed, and really quite sloppy. Their conclusion? That you're not much of a sociologist if you pass around such crap. And what if they tell that to others?

But say you can convince them that a working first draft is indeed a working draft, that it has been whapped out in a stream of consciousness fashion, that it is truly just for ideas. It's still terribly risky because the reader may not be looking for great grammar and well-turned phrases, but she is looking for stunning ideas. In some ways this is even more terrifying. It's ideas that are on the line, not ability to write. How often have you heard someone say, "Well, she may not be able to write, but god, is she brilliant!" It is OK to write like a college sophomore if you are bright. If you give someone a working draft to read, what you're asking them to do is pass judgment on your ability to think sociologically. You're asking them to decide whether you are smart or not and whether or not you are a real sociologist. If there are no flashes of insight, no riveting ideas, what will the reader conclude? That you're stupid. If she tells that to anyone else, it's the kiss of death. Hence the fear of letting anyone see working drafts. I cannot face the possibility of people thinking I'm stupid.

Most of these points also apply to letting sociologists other than your peers see your work, but with something of a twist. There are times when giving your work to senior colleagues seems even more dangerous than giving it to peers. Say you're an untenured faculty member. What is the practical outcome of getting known as a sloppy worker (scenario 1 above), or a concrete brain (scenario 2)? What if members of the tenured faculty reach this conclusion about you and your work? No grants, no job offers, no promotions. That's risky. Professional reputation is tied to professional position, and few of us have the power to say, "I don't care what you think."

To overcome these fears, to take the risk of being thought sloppy or stupid, you have to trust your colleagues. But the discipline is organized in a way that undermines that trust at every turn. Your peers are competing with you psychologically (ah, the perversity that allows me to feel better when someone else eats dirt) and structurally. Tenure, grants, goodies are becoming more and more part of a zero-sum game, as the academic world feels the current economic crunch.

So peers are hard to trust, especially those close to you: those in your department or those in your specialty. It's also very easy to fear your senior colleagues because you feel that they are constantly judging you. They're supposed to, because they are the ones who feel that they have the duty to weed out the good from the bad in this young crop of academics. They do talk to one another about your work and tell one another what they think of your potential. So how can you trust them not to tell tales when they decide that your work isn't very good?

This problem of trust is critical because it undermines the kind of emotional and intellectual freedom that we all need if we are to create. Who can you trust? I imagine there are a few people who are so confident that they don't really worry about what colleagues think, but they're a special breed, a very uncommon type. They just charge ahead, dropping off manuscripts left and right, filling up people's mailboxes with page after page of interesting and useful ideas. How is it possible? Some of them have the kind of personality that gives them this ability; others (most) have the structural freedom that gives them more power to say, "I don't give a damn what sociologists are 'supposed' to do, I'm doing what I want." I've noticed a little bit of this (a very little bit, I'm afraid) in myself now that I have tenure. It's not that I necessarily trust anyone more, it's just that I can be less concerned about the impact of their negative judgments.

But trust—. Who can you trust? When I think about the people I trust to read my work, I realize that they are people who already know how stupid I can be: the people I went to graduate school with, the people who taught me sociology while I was in graduate school, and a few people since that time whom I have come to know as friends as well as colleagues. People who knew me in graduate school have seen it all, and I know that with them there's only one way I can go: up. They've seen my early attempts to write and think, supported me through that, and believed that there was something lurking there beneath all the confusion. So I trust them. And, not incidentally, they trust me. We share things back and forth because of those early bonds. After all, nothing could rival the pain involved in those first attempts to sneak out into the world, scribble a few notes, and then come home and try to make something of it. And nothing can rival the exhilaration of having someone tell you that those tiny, tentative offerings were *good*. The colleagues since then who have also become friends are few but precious. Our mutual trust comes from having struggled to overcome the structural barriers that originally divided us. Like all friendships, they're the product of those cautious little dance steps that move you close together and then apart, near again and then farther away, each approach creating a bit more trust and concern. I have no prescription for creating those trusting friendships, though I wish I did. With me it's highly idiosyncratic, although it sometimes comes from working on a shared research project.

So these are the people I trust with working drafts. The professional risk is minimized by our common history. Their responses to me do something important, something absolutely critical if I am going to be able to continue to construct working drafts. Their responses convince me to trust myself, because for me, there's another great risk involved in writing. It's the risk of discovering that I am incapable of doing sociology and, by extension, that I am not a sociologist and therefore not the person I claim to be. The risk of being found out and judged by colleagues is bound up in the risk of being found out and judged by myself. The two are so closely interwoven that it is often hard for me to separate them. How can you know that you are doing OK, that you are a sociologist, unless someone tells you so? It's other people's responses that enable me to understand who I am.

These then are the twists of risk: I trust myself (and can therefore risk writing down my ideas—things that I have made up) primarily because others I trust have told me that I am OK. But no one can tell me that until I actually do something, until I actually write something down. So there I am, faced with a blank page, confronting the risk of discovering that I cannot do what I set out to do, and therefore am not the person I pretend to be. I haven't yet written anything, so no one can help me affirm my commitment and underscore my sense of who I am.

I need to mention something else about gathering confidence from the feedback of trusted friends. You have to trust these people not just to treat you right (not to be competitive with you, not to tell tales when you mess up), but also to tell you the truth. I must believe *absolutely* that if I write crap or think idiotic thoughts they will tell me. If I can't trust them to tell me the truth, then their feedback will not help me trust myself. I'll always wonder whether my ideas are really good, or whether they're just trying to be nice. The feeling that someone is humoring me is more damaging to my sense of self than outright attack. Sure, we all tell little white lies to each other. But there's got to be an underlying honesty, or I really start spinning. We must believe that it's no sin to make mistakes and no sin to criticize, otherwise feedback is useless.

How do I try to deal with all this risk and get myself moving? To begin writing at all, I sometimes have to look backward. I say to myself, "Well, I may not have written about prisons before, but I did write about juvenile delinquents, and people seem to think that was acceptable." It's at least a small bit of comfort. Or I look far to the future: I call trusted friends and tell them about my work. I run on and on, they make appropriately comforting noises, and then I feel a bit stronger. Sometimes I feel strong enough to begin writing. There's something that I think many of us believe: talking about work is less of a risk than writing about it. In part that's because no one remembers the ideas that you speak. But it's also as if we have an informal agreement not to hold one another responsible for anything we say. So I can throw out some safe comments, gather reinforcement, feel better about myself, and maybe take that first risk. But there is a catch here too. Because what we say doesn't count, it is easy to think of these conversations as inconsequential bull. But if I think that, then the listener's positive feedback is not credible, because I conclude she is responding to my act, my sociologist's facade, rather than to any meaningful ideas. If, however, I can learn to take talk seriously, people's responses can help me get the first words down on the page.

In some ways, writing gets easier the more you do it,

because the more you do it, the more you learn that it's really not as risky as you fear. You have a history on which to draw for self confidence, you have a believable reputation among a wider number of people whom you can call on the phone, and best of all, you have demonstrated to yourself that taking the risk can be worth it. You took the risk, produced something, and *voila!* Proof that you are who you claim to be. Though I must also admit that it's not as easy as I'm making it sound. My writing history gives me some confidence, but I look at my past work with mixed emotions. It looks awkward and full of errors, and I tell myself that I must do better. My expectations change constantly, and I continually redefine what I consider to be good work. This means that every time I sit down to write I find myself wondering whether I can really do this stuff at all. So writing is still a risky activity.

But what I seem to be learning as I spend more time writing is that the risks are worth taking. Yes, I produce an appalling amount of crap, but most of the time I can tell it's crap before anyone else gets a chance to look at it. And occasionally I produce something that fits, something Lillian Hellman might have written, something that captures exactly what I want to say. Usually it's just a sentence or two, but the number of those sentences grows if I just keep plugging away. This small hoard of good stuff also helps me take risks. When I feel as if I simply cannot write, I sometimes go back and reread sections of something I've written that I like. It reminds me that there are two sides to risk. You can lose, but you can also win. I tend to think only of losing, and that makes me fearful. Rereading some good stuff can sometimes get me started when other stratagems fail. And I'm also seeing that the negative side of risk-taking isn't as bad as I fear. I can hide the worst of the writing I do. No one besides me need ever see it— and I throw it out as quickly as I can. What I show others are things that I think have some merit, and even the occasional paragraph that rolls beautifully off the platen. In other words, I have some degree of control over the risks involved in writing and letting others see what I have done. I am not completely at anyone's mercy, not even the mercy of my own impossible demands for perfection. I am allowed to throw things away.

So. But it's the complexity of risk, its dual nature, that allows me to dream of being attacked by a friend and of writing like Lillian Hellman, both in the same night. As I write more and more, I begin to understand that it's not all-or-nothing. If I actually write something down, I'm liable to win a bit and lose a bit. For a long time I worked under the burden of thinking that it was an all-or-nothing proposition. What got written had to be priceless literary pearls or unmitigated garbage. Not so. It's just a bunch of stuff, more or less sorted into an argument. Some of it's good, some of it isn't.

I have nothing to add to this analysis. Pamela Richards has explored in detail the organization of peers and superiors characteristic of the world of the young academic and shown vividly how it affects one's willingness to take the chances that trying to be a professional intellectual confront you with. Having two personal stories in this book gives you a feel for what is peculiar to the person and what is generic in the situation and process. I don't know how typical these feelings are of other fields. I think they afflict most academics and intellectuals.

Seven

Getting It out the Door

Tracy Kidder's *The Soul of a New Machine*, an
account of an engineering team creating a new mini-
computer, taught me a useful expression: "getting it out
the door." People in the computer industry commonly
use it to refer to the final stage in the development of a
new product. It takes a long time to create a new
product: conceive the idea for it; translate the idea into
plans for hardware and get the hardware built; simultaneously create a software operating system to control
the hardware and the applications and programs that
will make the machine worth having built; write the
instruction manuals from which people will learn how
to use it; shrink wrap the books and disks; and finally
see the product shipped out to dealers and users.

The industry has a special expression for completing
the process because so many things can interfere with it
happening. Many projects never get out of the door.
The hardware doesn't work the way it's supposed to.

Suppliers don't deliver the components they promised to have ready. But new computers often don't get out of the door because the engineers who work on them don't think they are ready for release. The engineers are often right. The industry resounds with cautionary tales of machines released before they were ready, bankrupting companies, ruining the image of an essentially good product, and the reputations and careers of the people associated with it.

A common, superficially correct explanation attributes these disasters to a chronic tension between marketing people and engineers. Marketing people need the machine *now*. The competition has one, and the company will lose its share of the market if it doesn't bring out something similar soon. But the engineers know that with just a little more time they can make a better machine: freer of bugs, simpler and cleaner, more elegant, more completely embodying the vision they began with. They know that other engineers, if no one else, will appreciate those refinements and admire their ingenuity. The marketing people don't care about the elegance and perfection that impresses the engineers' peers. They think engineers are impractical cuckoos who would just as soon bankrupt the company by pursuing perfectionist pipe dreams. The marketers' operating standard is that the machine should be "plenty good enough," able to do the job it was designed for well enough to satisfy users. The rare engineer who successfully straddles the two worlds and integrates their differing standards commands everyone's respect as someone who can "get it out the door."

The tension between making it better and getting it done appears wherever people have work to finish or a product to get out: a computer, a dinner, a term paper, an automobile, a book. We want to get it done and out to the people who will use it, eat it, read it. But no object ever fully embodies its maker's conception of what it could have been. Human frailty, your own and that of others, makes flaws and mistakes inevitable. You forget to put in the salt, overlook some important bug in your program, commit a logical fallacy, leave out an important variable, write a shamefully awkward sentence, ignore the relevant scholarly literature, misinterpret your data—every form of production has its list of common mistakes. But maybe, we think, if I just go over it one more time, I can catch those mistakes and devise even better solutions to the problems I set out to solve.

Getting it out the door is not the only thing people value. A lot of important work in a lot of of fields has been done with little regard for whether it ever got out the door. Scholars and artists, especially, believe that if they wait long enough they may find a more comprehensive and logical way to say what they think. The same attitude finds an honored place in professional folklore and tradition. The American composer Charles Ives just didn't care, in the later stages of his composing career, whether anything ever got out the door. His reputation rests on works he never considered completed, although they were, in some sense, but not *his*, done. In fact, little of his music would have been played had not determined players bullied and wheedled until he reluctantly let them have the scores. Even then, he gave them little help deciphering the complexities and ambiguities of his scrawls (see the accounts in Perlis 1974).

Makers often want to delay getting the product out the door, even when (as in the scholarly world) the creator is also the marketing division and knows exactly why it *must* get out, and soon. Some authors' work leaves their desks only when someone steals it. A publisher I knew went to an author's house and, with the collusion of the author's wife, stole a manuscript the author thought still needed a little more work, especially on the footnotes. The author did not complain when the book came out.

For writers, getting it out the door occurs in several

steps. Their work goes through the first door when they show it to a circle of trusted friends and colleagues for comments and suggestions. Further doors lead to course instructors, thesis advisers, journal referees, publishers' readers, and eventually to the great anonymous public who can read the work once it is publicly available. Some writers first get hung up while still students, failing to turn in course papers on time and accumulating record numbers of incompletes. Some let their trusted friends see work only when isolation makes them desperate, and then give them highly polished, heavily reworked materials. Others show friends early versions, but balk at submitting anything for publication, insisting that they need to reread a few of the great masters, run a few more tables, spend a little more time on their bibliography—whatever excuse their work makes plausible.

I like to get it out the door. Although I like to rewrite and tinker with organization and wording, I soon either put work aside as not ready to be written or get it into a form fit to go out the door. My temperament—impatient, eager for frequent rewards, curious about how others will respond to what I have said—pushes me in that direction. Growing up in the popular music business, where you play every night whether you feel like it or not, whether or not what you play is as good as it can be, probably reinforces my temperament. Most importantly, Everett Hughes taught me that intellectual life is a dialogue among people interested in the same topic. You can eavesdrop on the conversation and learn from it, but eventually you ought to add something yourself. Your research project isn't done until you have written it up and launched it into the conversation by publishing it. That view has obvious roots in the pragmatic philosophy of John Dewey and George Herbert Mead, both influential in sociological thought and practice. It also has heavily moralistic overtones.

Students and colleagues who have worked with me know just how moralistic, stubborn, and irritating I can

be about getting it out the door. Why don't they finish
their theses? Where is that chapter they promised?
You're almost done—*what's taking so long?* I know,
when I get like that, that I am overlooking something.
Nothing is ever so simple, so either/or. So I look for the
rest of the story. There is always more.

I found the other side of this story, following the
computer metaphor, by asking whether you could get
the product out the door too soon. The question answers itself. Computer businesses ruin themselves by
ignoring the engineers' warnings. But it goes beyond
that. James Joyce was in no hurry to get *Finnegan's
Wake* out the door. Many masterpieces result from
years of patient reworking by people who seem not to
care whether the damn thing gets done. At an extreme,
exemplified by Ives, producers stop caring whether
they ever finish anything. Some masterpieces, to be
sure, get done quickly, but the chance that a little more
work might turn good into great ought to slow anyone
down. Working slowly, sacrificing present rewards to
produce something really valuable, spending twenty
years to produce one book (as John Rawls did with *A
Theory of Justice*)—it's an appealing image, even to
someone as practical as me.

So "get it out" and "wait a while" both have a lot to
recommend them. The conventional (and only sensible) solution to such a problem is to see that you are
choosing between competing goods and try to balance
them. But that recognition doesn't help much. Where
should we strike the balance? It's the same problem.

The case of Ives suggests an approach. How could he
be a composer and yet never finish a composition? He
did it by being a certain kind of composer: one whose
music was not played. Music that hasn't been finished
can't be played. Players can, of course, take your score
away from you and finish it by fiat, as they did to Ives.
But Ives didn't have to finish anything because he had
chosen not to participate in the standard forms of
cooperative activity, in the conversation, of the music

business of his day. Not caring whether his music was played or not, he had no need to finish it.

More generally, you can decide when to let your work out the door by deciding what part you want to play in the world in which work like yours is done. Saying that does not merely translate an insoluble question into another language, leaving it equally intractable. The new wording at least makes you think about and take into account the organizational rewards and punishments of different strategies.

When I talk with graduate students who have stalled on a dissertation, or academic friends who can't write their research up or put articles into publishable form, I should stop moralizing and talk instead about social organization. Unless I sit on the preacher in me firmly, however, our talks degenerate into unresolvable and irritating moralistic arguments. I begin lecturing them not to be perfectionists, to settle for what is good enough for the rest of us. I tell them I have never written a masterpiece and don't ever expect to. What makes them different?

They don't like that. Why should they? They often don't recognize or accept the diagnosis, which may well be wrong, and then get equally moralistic. Getting things done just to be getting them done does not seem very principled. In fact, it smacks of careerism. Academicians often speculate that people who "publish a lot" do so for unsavory reasons.

To understand the argument I've just described, we need to drop the moralism and see the problem in relation to the social organization of academic life. C. Wright Mills's conception of the *vocabulary of motives* (1940) helps here. Every society or social group has a list of understandable and acceptable reasons for doing things. Thus, we can explain that we took a particular job because we "needed the money," or "like working with people," or are "interested in that kind of stuff," or because "it has opportunities for advancement." Those are all understandable reasons for doing things in contemporary America. We may not do things for such reasons, or approve of anyone doing so, but we understand that others who do are neither crazy nor evil. In other societies, people might explain that they did something because their mother's brother said they had to, or because God told them to. Some friends would understand my deciding to take a new job because I'm an Aries and that's the way Aries are. But I would have to be very careful who heard me say I did it because God told me to.

We don't use our society's list of acceptable explanations only to talk to other people. We also ask ourselves why we do things and look for reasonable explanations in the same list. If we can't find one, we may not do what we had in mind, or we may wonder about our sanity. Who does things for no reason?

The vocabulary of motives current in academia explains frequent scholarly publishing in a variety of ways, many unflattering. People do it to "get ahead," "make a reputation," "get a raise" and, saddest of all, "to get tenure." Such reasons imply that the author settles for second-best, accepts work that is "good enough" just to get the result out the door and collect the reward.

Scholars who do get things done in a "reasonable time" find that analysis self-serving, an excuse for not finishing. They explain that they write "to contribute to science," "to take part in the scholarly dialogue," or because "writing is fun." I talk that way. These reasons sound Pollyannaish, and a little unbelievable. (People who suffer when they write find the idea that writing is fun particularly preposterous.) Nevertheless, some writers do things for these reasons. If you think of scholarly activity as a big game, then writing something, getting into the dialogue, or making a contribution can all be at least as much fun as clearing a PacMan screen. If, however, you focus on getting things right, then this emphasis on production smells of compromise. The rhetoric sounds self-serving, even immoral.

Such a moral duel leads nowhere. It's more useful to talk about the consequences of different ways of writing. In fact, the organization of academic life evokes and rewards both sets of motives, makes both of them reasonable and necessary.

How is the world of scholarship organized, and what part does writing and publishing play in it? What part do you want to play in it, and how will the way you write and publish affect whether you can play the part you have chosen? Good questions, for which, not surprisingly, there are no solid answers. Not surprisingly, because academics are as unwilling as others to study the organization of their social world. They don't want their secrets exposed or their favorite myths revealed as fairy tales. They like to tell stories of their experiences and draw vast conclusions from them about what makes students tick, what career strategies work (I've done both in this book), and especially, how "rational" the governing of universities is despite the surface appearance of chaos. Systematic investigation of students, careers, or universities would surely violate their convictions, and so no one thinks it worth doing or cooperating with.

Thus no body of research exists to settle these questions. Still, we can make some beginnings. Little of what I say will be controversial. Like so much other knowledge of how society works, people really knew it all along, but would rather not have to think about the implications and corollaries. The sociologist's job is to say such things out loud and make everyone think about them seriously.

Scholarly worlds embody a deep ambivalence, mirrored in the opposing attitudes of get-it-out versus take-your-time. On their practical side, worlds of scholarship are what Everett Hughes (1971, 52–64) called "going concerns," oriented toward getting work done. Less practically, they take the long view of history, looking toward the development, over years, even centuries, of a body of practice and knowledge. In the practical mode, they are in business right now and have to deal with all the immediate problems of any going concern. They may not have to produce a new computer in order to keep a share of the market (although the competition for student enrollments, academic reputation, and money is somewhat analogous). But they give birth to and support formal associations, which have annual meetings and publish journals, which in turn require that people write papers for oral delivery and publication. Scholarly worlds provide the pool of labor which staffs university departments and teaches their courses. Scholarly worlds produce the textbooks from which those courses are taught. Their members give interviews to newspapers and testify to legislatures on divorce, crime, nuclear power, natural disasters, or whatever the discipline is supposed to know enough to talk about.

Most of these activities require that someone get some writing done, some product out the door. The organization of scholarly disciplines does not require any particular person to do these jobs. If I don't write a definitive book on the subject, you will; if not you, someone else. If neither of us writes the book, we may suffer; but the field will not. We will not be promoted, but someone will eventually write it, if the material to write it from exists, and they will get promoted while we continue to teach the introductory course.

Nevertheless, those activities open the doors through which our scholarly writing can be moved out. Professionals orient themselves to the deadlines and constraints the disciplines create. Practical, they compromise. They will not, for instance, write in formats that are too short or too long for the standard media in which their work might appear. They can achieve a reputation, like that of the engineers who get computers out the door, for producing what is needed, in the form it is needed in, on time. From this perspective, it is easy to dismiss problems of writing, as I'm told one professor does when he explains to his graduate students that all they have to do is copy what appears in the *American Sociological Review*. If you use the major journals as exemplars (in one of the senses that Thomas Kuhn used that term) you will have problems only until you have mastered the form. From then on, writing should be as effortless as typing.

The scholarly world—this is the other side of the ambivalence—is also oriented toward the long run. In that mode, it does not need more of the same. It needs new ideas. But the old formats make it hard for a different idea to get a breath. Erving Goffman was both stubborn and good enough to make professional gatekeepers accept the pieces he wrote in totally "impractical" lengths: sixty page essays, too long for journals and too short for a book. Most people do not produce such strikingly original work and do not have the personal force which made his quixotic enterprises successful. But people who "take forever" to finish what they write are not as crazy, lazy, or self-indulgent as people like me make them out to be. They have simply oriented themselves toward the long run, in which meeting ephemeral deadlines for the sessions of the Midwest Sociological Society is really trivial and not worth bothering about. That is not foolish.

For the discipline as a whole, this is undoubtedly a good thing. So long as some people do one thing and some do the other, the various activities through which the scholarly world does what we expect it to do—teach classes, put out journals, create new ideas—all get done. But individuals may suffer by virtue of which of the world's jobs they take on. If you take twenty years to write a book which then turns out not to be a major intellectual event, you will certainly suffer. But if enough people try, the scholarly world will benefit. If we make that choice, we're playing for big stakes in a risky game and ought to recognize it.

A few assumptions, which ought to be made explicit and checked for accuracy, underly these analyses. People assume, for instance, that taking more time is necessarily better than taking less time. After all, shouldn't thinking about a topic for a year produce better ideas and deeper understanding? Won't the extra time allow you to polish your prose so that it more accurately and elegantly expresses your improved thoughts? Of course these benefits will follow! The more time you invest, the greater your return.

Writers who balk at working quickly and getting the product out the door also think that masterpieces take a long time to do, while pulp-magazine writers get their work done quickly. Who wouldn't prefer to write a masterpiece as opposed to a pulp-magazine piece? It's a questionable comparison. Should we try to write great masterpieces, or would we be better off aiming for good, clear prose that says what needs to be said in a way that is convincing? Does science need masterworks of prose? What chance does something written in the conventional style of the scholarly journals have of being a masterpiece? The pretentiousness of the ambition won't stand a close look. Besides, the authors of the great masterpieces of Victorian fiction—Dickens, Thackeray, Eliot, Trollope—wrote them under the conditions of pulp-magazine writing, as chapters of serials that might not even have been finished if the early numbers had not sold (Sutherland 1976).

Equating time spent and quality may in fact be empirically false. Painting teachers encourage students not to overpaint a picture, continuing to put paint on the canvas until an initially good idea is buried in a muddy mess. Writers can worry a piece to death, fussing over adjectives and word order until readers respond to the effort that went into the polishing more than to the thought the prose was supposed to convey. More work may not produce a better product. On the contrary, the more we think about it, the more we may introduce irrelevant considerations and inappropriate qualifications, insist on making connections that needn't be made—until we bury the thought in Byzantine ornamentation. "More is better" is no more true than "less is better." Yes, writing needs reworking and thought. But how much? The answer should be sought pragmatically, not in fixed attitudes.

A related assumption, whose puritanical bases are obvious, is that you ought to work hard on your writing, and that you do that by putting in long hours. Even if you don't actually write, you should at least sit at your desk and try. Suffer, if you can't write. Such Calvinism might result from lower-school training, from teachers who insist that you look like you're working even if you don't get anything done, that you at least not enjoy yourself doing something else when you should be working. Writers who accept that dutifully give themselves backaches by staring into space from an uncomfortable chair while they try to figure out what to say or how to improve how they have said it. But staring into space doesn't really look like working, and even the unproductive author eventually realizes it isn't effective.

Classic descriptions of writing problems frequently include a touching account of a sheet of white paper that begs to be written on, while the author confronting it sits frozen with anxiety. Every word seems wrong. Not only do the words seem wrong, they also seem dangerous. In chapter 6 Pamela Richards explored the fear of the potentially dangerous reactions of peers, superiors, and oneself that the organization of scholarly life produces. (I knew someone who would not get out of his pajamas until the first page of an article seemed perfect to him. He often used as many as a hundred sheets of paper trying to get the first sentence right, and finally had to give up the practice when he found himself still in bedclothes at dinner time.)

Another kind of anxiety that deserves exploration was mentioned in chapter 1. It still afflicts me. Scholars know that the subjects they write about involve so much that ought to be considered, so many connections between so many elements, so much of everything that it seems inconceivable that it can be given a rational order. But that's our business: to arrange ideas in so rational an order that another person can make sense of them. We have to deal with that problem on two levels. We have to arrange the ideas in a theory or narrative, describe the causes and conditions that lead to the effects we want to explain, and do it in an order that is logically and empirically correct (if we are writing something based on empirical research). Logically correct means that we haven't committed any of the well-known fallacies of incorrect reasoning (Fischer 1970 describes historians committing all of these fallacies). Empirically correct means that the order we describe should be the order that things really have in nature, as best we know it. Finally, we want our prose to make the order we have constructed clear. We don't want imperfections in our prose to interfere with our readers' understanding.

These two jobs converge and cannot be separated. I shouldn't say that so blithely. It is probably possible to outline and construct an argument in some other language than verbal. Mathematics and graphics are two alternatives that allow precise statement, and someone might work out a theory in one of those ways and not be able to put it into words. In any event, getting ideas in logical order requires a keen eye for fallacious arguments. One can learn to spot such errors. It is more frightening to try to describe empirical order accurately. We know we cannot describe everything. In fact, one aim of science and scholarship is exactly to reduce what has to be described to manageable proportions. But what to leave out? And where should we put what we leave in? The empirical world may be ordered, but not in any simple way that dictates which topics should be taken up first. That's why people stare at blank sheets of paper and rewrite first sentences a hundred times. They want those mystical exercises to flush out the One Right Way of organizing all that stuff.

Well, what if you don't get it organized properly? We looked at that problem in chapter 3. But what if (which is much worse), knowing that any organization of reality you make will likely be incorrect in some way, you don't get it organized at all? That is the deepest cause of the anxiety that strikes writers when they begin. What if we cannot, *just cannot*, make order out of that chaos? I don't know about other people, but beginning a new paper gives me anxiety's classical physical symptoms: dizziness, a sinking feeling in the pit of the stomach, a chill, maybe even a cold sweat. The dual possibilities, one as bad as the other, that the world has no real order or that, if it does, I can't find it, now or ever, are philosophically, almost religiously, frightening. The world may be a meaningless mess, but that is not a philosophical position one can live with easily. Not being able to figure out the first sentence makes that possibility palpable.

Do I have a cure for the disease I've described? Yes and no. A lot of other activities, especially sports, provoke paralyzing fears that keep people from getting started. The advice of experts in these areas is always the same. Relax and *do it!*. You cannot overcome the fear without doing the thing you are afraid of and finding out that it is not as dangerous as you imagined. So the solution for writing something that will not fully, logically, and completely master the chaos is to write it anyway and discover that the world will not end when you do. You might be able to do that by tricking yourself into thinking that what you are writing is unimportant and makes no difference—a letter to an old friend, perhaps. I know how to trick myself, but I don't know how others can trick themselves. So here is where the advice stops. You can't start swimming until you get in the water.

Eight

Terrorized by the Literature

S tudents (and others) often, as I said earlier, talk about "using" this or that approach—"I think I'll use Durkheim"—as though they had a free choice of theories. In fact, by the time they begin to write about their research, they have made many seemingly unimportant choices of details that have foreclosed their choice of a theoretical approach. They decided what questions to investigate. They picked a way of gathering information. They chose between a variety of minor technical and procedural alternatives: who to interview, how to code their data, when to stop. As they made these choices from day to day, they increasingly committed themselves to one way of thinking, more or less firmly answering the theoretical questions they thought were still up for grabs.

But sociologists, and especially students, fuss about choosing a theory for a practical reason. They have to— at least they think they do—deal with the "literature" on their topic. Scholars learn to fear the literature in graduate school. I remember Professor Louis Wirth, one of the distinguished members of the Chicago school, putting Erving Goffman, then a fellow graduate student of mine, in his place with the literature gambit. It was just what we all feared. Believing Wirth had not given sufficiently serious attention to some influential ideas about operationalism, Goffman challenged him in class with quotations from Percy Bridgeman's book on the subject. Wirth smiled and asked sadistically, "Which edition is that, Mr. Goffman?" Maybe there was an important difference between editions, though none of us believed that. We thought, instead, that we'd better be careful about the literature or They Could Get You. "They" included not only teachers but peers, who might welcome an opportunity to show how well they knew the literature at your expense.

Students learn that they must say something about all the people who have discussed "their" problem before them. No one wants to discover that their carefully nurtured idea was in print before they thought of it (maybe before they were born) and in a place they should have looked. (Wirth also told us that originality was the product of a faulty memory.) Students want to show the world, and all the critics who may be out there laying for them, that they have looked and that no one has had their idea before.

A good way to prove your originality is to attach your idea to a tradition in which people have already explored the literature. Hitching your work to a well-explored scholarly star helps you to assure yourself that your work doesn't redo something already done. If you "use" Weber or Durkheim or Marx or Mead, the exegetes have preceded you, laying out the terrain, specifying what the questions really are, defining what work by who will be relevant to consider—and in general providing a surefire way of dealing with the literature: "See Chaim Yankel's exhaustive review (1993) of the literature in this area." This protective ritual effectively covers the author's ass, but works less well to produce good or interesting scholarship. The reasons, interesting in themselves, also illuminate the institutional bases of creativity and banality.

Writers should, of course, use relevant literature appropriately. Stinchcombe (1982) has pointed out six major uses. (I intend my summary of his paper to exemplify what I will describe later as a good use of the literature, to provide an already thought-through piece of an argument you need.) Although Stinchcombe writes about the narrower category of "classics," what he has to say also speaks to our problem of "the literature."

Two of the six uses he discusses relate to early phases of research and are less relevant to problems of writing. As a source of fundamental ideas, the classics are very important in the early stages of a project; but by the time you start writing, you ought to have your fundamental ideas clear. Clear or not, you already have them and they have informed your work and done their best or worst. The classics' second function, as "under-exploited normal science," as a source of empirical hypotheses, hunches, and hints, is similarly crucial in the prewriting stages. Stinchcombe also mentions an organizational function of the classics: to symbolize solidarity among people in a field. "It is the fact that we have all read these classics, or at least answered preliminary examination questions on them, that binds us together into an intellectual community." He worries about this function, thinking that it leads us to admire work that time may have shown to be wrong (as, he says, Whitney Pope showed that Durkheim was wrong about suicide): "What is destructive about admiration of the classics, then, is the halo effect, the belief that because a book or article is useful for one purpose, it must have all the virtues."

Three other important uses of the classics have directly to do with getting our writing done. A classic work of scholarship serves as a touchstone: "a concrete example of the virtues scientific work might have, in a combination that shows what work should look like in order to contribute to the discipline." As Stinchcombe says, this is what Thomas Kuhn meant when he used the term *paradigm* in the sense of an exemplar. The virtues Stinchcombe is talking about are not the ones you might expect:

> [F]irst class science functions with aesthetic standards as well as with logical and empirical standards. These standards are not defensible by the positivist or the Marxist or the symbolic interactionist philosophies of science. . . . [I]f we embed the examples of excellence in our minds, as concrete manifestations of aesthetic principles we want to respect in our own work, and use them as touchstones to filter out that part we throw away and that part we keep, we may very well manage to work at a level higher than we can teach. For we work by the standards embedded in the touchstone, standards we cannot formulate but can perceive if we use a paired comparison— is this piece as good as Simmel?

Stinchcombe here describes what I meant when I spoke earlier of editing by ear. If he is right, and these aesthetic standards cannot be justified "scientifically," it follows that there is no sense trying to find the One Right Way to write what you have to say. Copying well-done work (especially its organization or format), however, is a wonderful way to find possible right ways.

Classics also serve as "developmental tasks for novices," showing them how much more complicated things are than they thought and bringing them up to the level of sophistication common in their field. This function is usually what people have in mind when they talk about the benefits of studying for qualifying exams. It probably contributes to the irrational way people think about the literature, and to the mindlessly ritualistic literature reviews that decorate so much scholarly work.

Stinchcombe calls a final use of the classics "intellectual small change." You cite Weber or Durkheim or Yankel (just as you use the catchwords of a school) to show what camp you belong to. To do this, you must use well known names:

> Imagine if our badges for the convention [he is referring to the annual meeting of the American Sociological Association] had our names, our institutions, and our favorite classic writer. So mine might read "Stinchcombe, University of Arizona, Max Weber." Suppose now, in a fit of preciousness, I write instead "Stinchcombe, University of Arizona, Paul Veyne." He is right now the person I am most intellectually excited about, and embodies the same virtues as Max Weber. But 90–odd per cent of the people I met would not know who I was talking about, so would not learn anything about the set of prejudices and intuitions to which I was declaring my loyalty. . . . [But] the use of classics as identifying badges tends to produce sects rather than open intellectual communities. The badges tend to become boundaries rather than guides.

The conventional review of the literature provides evidence of the author's allegiances in this way, but authors would be briefer and less obsessive if that were their main purpose.

The classics are not the same as "the literature." Sociologists worry about the classics, but they also worry about the literature of commentary and methodological discussion, about research reporting specific findings on the topic and discussions of those findings, all of which they feel responsible for (much as students know when they are "responsible" for material on a test).

None of these are intrinsically bad ways to use the literature, but none of them answers the question of how to use the literature on your research topic.

Science and humanistic scholarship are, in fact as well as in theory, cumulative enterprises. None of us invent it all from scratch when we sit down to write. We depend on our predecessors. We couldn't do our work if we didn't use their methods, results, and ideas. Few people would be interested in our results if we didn't indicate some relationship between them and what others have said and done before us. Kuhn (1962) spoke of this mutual dependence and cumulation as "normal science." Many sociologists use "normal science" pejoratively, as though it meant "*merely* normal science," as though all of us could expect to produce scientific revolutions every day. That is a total misreading of Kuhn, and foolishness as well. Individual scientists don't make scientific revolutions. Those revolutions take a long time. Large numbers of people, working together, develop a new way of formulating and investigating the problems they are interested in, a way which finds a home in lasting institutions of scientific work. To imagine that your report of your project will accomplish what takes all that time and all those people is wrong-headed. It's alright to aim for the stars, but we ought to have a decent regard for what is humanly possible. If making a scientific or scholarly revolution singlehandedly is our chief goal, we are bound to fail. Better to pursue the goals of normal science: to do a piece of good work others can use, and thus increase knowledge and understanding. Since we can attain those things in our own research and writing, we don't set ourselves up for failure by aiming at the impossible.

A scholar can try to work in isolation from others and without their help, like so-called naive artists who produce paintings and constructions without reference to any of the traditions of the medium they work in. Artists who do that usually produce exceptionally eccentric work, but their work is also free of the constraints imposed by standard ways of working. That freedom from organizational constraint sometimes allows naive artists to produce works which command the respect of an established art world and which may even eventually be absorbed into its tradition. The dialectic of constraint and opportunity that naive artists illustrate affects all of us as we write our dissertations, papers, and books. That dialectic suggests two questions: how we can use the literature effectively? How does the literature get in our way and prevent us from doing our best work?

Are there effective ways to use the literature? Of course. For one thing, scholars must say something new while connecting what they say to what's already been said, and this must be done in such a way that people will understand the point. They must say something at least minimally new. Although the empirical sciences pay lip service to the idea of replicating results, they don't pay off for it. At the same time, as you approach total originality, you interest fewer and fewer people. Everyone is interested in the topics people have studied and written about for years, both because the topics are of great and continuing general concern (why do people commit suicide?) and because they have been studied for so long that they have created the kind of scientific puzzles Kuhn (1962) identified with normal science (the literature investigating Durkheim's theory of suicide exemplifies this). The ideal scholarly contribution makes readers say: "That's interesting!" As Michael Schudson suggested to me, students must learn to connect their work to the literature in just that way, to set their results in the context of accepted theories that make it unlikely (see Davis 1971 and Polya 1954).

I remarked earlier that my use of Stinchcombe's article exemplifies what I think is a better way to use what others have done. Here's what I meant. Imagine that you are doing a woodworking project, perhaps making a table. You have designed it and cut out some of the parts. Fortunately, you needn't make all the parts yourself. Some are standard sizes and shapes—lengths of two by four, for instance—available at any lumberyard. Some have already been designed and made by other people—drawer pulls and turned legs. All you have to do is fit them into the places you left for them, knowing that they were available. That is the best way to use the literature. You want to make an argument, instead of a table. You have created some of the argument yourself, perhaps on the basis of new data or information you have collected. But you needn't invent the whole thing. Other people have worked on your problem or problems related to it and have made some of the pieces you need. You just have to fit them in where they belong. Like the woodworker, you leave space, when you make your portion of the argument, for the other parts you know you can get. You do that, that is, *if* you know that they are there to use. And that's one good reason to know the literature: so that you will know what pieces are available and not waste time doing what has already been done.

Here's an example. When I was working on the theory of deviance (eventually published in *Outsiders* (1963)), I wanted to argue that when others labeled someone as a deviant, that identification often became the most important thing about the person so labeled. I could have worked out a theory about how that happened, but I didn't need to. Everett Hughes (1971, 141–50) had already developed a theory describing the way statuses develop a halo of "auxiliary status characteristics," so that we expect, for instance, an American Catholic priest to be "Irish, athletic, and a good sort who with difficulty refrains from profanity in the presence of evil and who may punch someone in the nose if the work of the Lord demands it." Or, to take a more serious example, although all you need in order to practice medicine is a license from the state, we commonly expect doctors to be white male Protestants of old American stock. Hughes was especially interested in the intersection of race and professional position and, in developing his argument, made the following observation:

> Membership in the Negro race, as defined in American mores or law, may be called a *master status-determining trait*. It tends to overpower, in most crucial situations, any other characteristics which might run counter to it. But professional standing is also a powerful characteristic—most so in the specific relationships of professional practice, less so in the general intercourse of people. (147, emphasis added)

The idea of a master status-determining trait, which takes precedence in identifying people socially, was no more than an aside in Hughes's article. If I were to write an article titled "The Sociological Thought of Everett C. Hughes," I would not spend much time on it. But in working out my theory, I wanted precisely to talk about how a disreputable status characteristic like being addicted to drugs could spoil reputable statuses—genius or priest or doctor or whatever—one might think would neutralize it. Hughes wanted to talk about how the status of Negro overpowered the status of doctor. I wanted to talk about how the status of junkie overpowered the status of son or husband, so that parents or spouses locked up the family silver and jewels when their beloved dope-fiend relative came to dinner. I wanted to talk about what a character in Doris Lessing's *The Four-Gated City* meant when she said that she didn't mind being thought schizophrenic but didn't like people to think that that was *all* she was.

Hughes's language fits my case exactly. I didn't need to invent the concept; he had invented it for me. So, instead of creating yet another unnecessary new sociological term, I quoted Hughes and went on to make more use of his idea than he had in the article I took it from. In the same way, I had no need to work out the uses of the classics. Stinchcombe had done it. I only had to quote and summarize.

Is working that way plagiarizing or being unoriginal? I don't think so, although fear of such labels pushes people to desperate attempts to think of new concepts. If I need the idea for the table I'm building, I'll take it. It's still my table, even though some parts were prefabricated.

In fact, I am so accustomed to working this way that I am always collecting such prefabricated parts for use in future arguments. Much of my reading is governed by a search for such useful modules. Sometimes I know I need a particular theoretical part and even have a good idea of where to find it (often thanks to my graduate training in theory, to say a good word for what I so often feel like maligning). When I wrote my dissertation about Chicago public school teachers, I found modules I needed in the writings of such classic sociologists as Georg Simmel and Max Weber. Discussing how teachers expected school principals to take their side of any argument with a student, whatever the facts of the case, I found a general description of the class that phenomenon belonged to in Simmel's essay on superiority and subordination: "The position of the subordinate in regard to his superordinate is favorable if the latter, in his turn, is subordinate to a still higher authority in which the former finds support" (Simmel 1950, 235). I also wanted to argue that the desire of school personnel to keep parents and the general public out of school affairs was a specific instance of a phenomenon important in organizations of all kinds. I found that module in Max Weber: "Bureaucratic administration always tends to be an administration of 'secret sessions'; in so far as it can, it hides its knowledge and action from criticism. . . . [T]he tendency toward secrecy in certain administrative fields follows their material nature: everywhere that the power inter-

ests of the dominant structure toward *the outside* are at
stake . . . we find secrecy" (Gerth and Mills 1946, 233).

On the other hand, I didn't know I needed the next
module until I found it; then I couldn't do without it. It
did not come from one of the conventionally recognized classics, although the work it is in is elegantly
excellent. Willard Waller helped me and my readers
understand why schools had a discipline problem
when he said: "Teacher and pupil confront each other
in the school with an original conflict of desires, and
however much that conflict may be reduced in amount,
or however much it may be hidden, it still remains"
(Waller 1932, 197).

I also collect modules I have no present use for,
when my intuition tells me I will eventually find the
use. Here are some ideas I have stored away recently,
expecting sometime to find a place for them in my
thinking and writing sometime: Raymonde Moulin's
(1967) idea that, in art works, economic and aesthetic
value are so closely related as to be the same thing, and
Bruno Latour's (1983, 1984) idea that scientific inven-
tions create new political forces, as Pasteur's work in
microbiology did by introducing the microbe as a social
actor. I may not use these ideas in their original form. I
may transform them in ways their parents wouldn't
recognize or approve of, and interpret them in ways
students of these thinkers will find incorrect. I will
probably use them in contexts quite different from
those in which they were first proposed, and fail to give
due weight to theoretical exegeses which strive to
discover the core meanings their inventors intended.
But I carry them with me, ready to apply when I make
my observations or begin writing. It will be easier to use
them, of course, if I have had them in mind all along.
But I may also find that I had some such idea in mind,
only not very clearly, and that Latour or Moulin or
Waller has done the hard work of clarification for me. I
am grateful, recognize that as part of the cooperative
work of scholarship, and cite and quote them in the

appropriate places. My work may look like a patchwork quilt as a result. When that happens I console myself with the example of Walter Benjamin, the German-Jewish man of letters, whose methods Hannah Arendt described this way:

> From the Goethe essay on, quotations are at the center of every work of Benjamin's. This very fact distinguishes his writings from scholarly works of all kinds in which it is the function of quotations to verify and document opinions, wherefore they can safely be relegated to the Notes. . . . The main work [for Benjamin] consisted in tearing fragments out of their context and arranging them afresh in such a way that they illustrated one another and were able to prove their *raison d'etre* in a free-floating state, as it were. It definitely was a sort of surrealistic montage. (Arendt 1969, 47)

That's the good side of the literature. The bad side is that paying too much attention to it can deform the argument you want to make. Suppose there is a *real* literature on your subject, the result of years of normal science or what, by extension, we could call normal scholarship. Everyone who works on the topic agrees on the kinds of questions to ask and the kinds of answers they will accept. If you want to write about the topic, or even use that subject matter as the material for a new topic, you will probably have to deal with the old way even though you think it quite foreign to your interests. If you take the old way too seriously, you can deform the argument you want to make, bend it out of shape in order to make it fit into the dominant approach.

What I mean by bending your argument out of shape is this. What you want to say has a certain logic that flows from the chain of choices you made as you did the work. If the logic of your argument is the same as the logic of the dominant approach to the topic, you have no problem. But suppose it isn't. What you want to say starts from different premises, addresses different questions, recognizes a different kind of answer as appropriate. When you try to confront the dominant approach to this material, you start to translate your argument into its terms. Your argument will not make the kind of sense it made in its own terms; it will sound weak and disjointed and will appear ad hoc. It cannot look its best playing an opponent's game. And that phrasing puts the point badly, because what's involved is not a contest between approaches, after all, but a search for a good way to understand the world. The understanding you're trying to convey will lose its coherence if it is put in terms that grow out of a different understanding.

If, on the other hand, you translate the dominant argument into your terms, you will not give it a fair shake, for much the same reasons. When you translate from one way of analyzing a problem into another, there is a good chance that the approaches are, as Kuhn (1962) suggested, incommensurable. Insofar as they address different questions, the approaches have very little to do with one another. There is nothing to translate. They are simply not talking about the same things.

The literature has the advantage of what is sometimes called ideological hegemony over you. If its authors own the territory, their approach to it seems as natural and reasonable as your new and different approach seems strange and unreasonable. Their ideology controls how readers think about the topic. As a result, you have to explain why you haven't asked those questions and gotten those answers. Proponents of the dominant argument don't have to explain their failure to look at things your way. (Latour and Bastide 1983 discuss this problem in the sociology of science.)

My work in deviance taught me this lesson the hard way. When I began studying marijuana use in 1951, the ideologically dominant question, the only question worth looking at, was "Why do people do a weird thing like that?" and the ideologically preferred way of answering it was to find a psychological trait or social attribute which differentiated people who did from people who didn't. The underlying premise was that "normal" people, who did not possess the distinguishing causal stigma you hoped to discover, would not do anything so bizarre. I started from a different premise: that "normal" people would do almost anything if the circumstances were right. That meant that you had to ask what situations and processes led people to change their minds about this activity and do what they formerly would not do.

The two ways of investigating marijuana use are not totally divergent. They can be made to coincide, and that's what I did when I first published the material in 1953: I made them coincide. I showed that users went through a process of redefining the drug experience that led them to regard it differently. Sociologists, psychologists, and others interested in drug use found that an interesting answer. It helped start a spate of studies of how people became this or that kind of deviant, mostly based on the premise that these were normal people who had just had some different experiences. Well, you might ask, what's wrong with that strategy?

What's wrong with it, something I did not realize until years later, is that my eagerness to show that this literature (dominated by psychiatrists and criminologists) was wrong led me to ignore what my research was really about. I had blundered onto, and then proceeded to ignore, a much larger and more interesting question: how do people learn to define their own internal experiences? That question leads to the exploration of how people define all sorts of internal states, and not just drug experiences. How do people know when they are hungry? That question has become of great interest to scientists who study obesity. How do people know when they are short of breath or have normal bowel movements or any of the other things doctors ask about in taking a medical history? Those questions interest medical sociologists. How do people know when they are "crazy"? I think, looking back, that my study would have made a more profound contribution if I had oriented it to those questions. But the ideological hegemony of the established way of studying drugs beat me.

I don't know how people can tell when they are letting the literature deform their argument. It is the classic dilemma of being trapped in the categories of your time and place. What you can do is recognize the dominant ideology (as I did at the time with respect to drug use), look for its ideological component, and try to find a more neutral scientific stance toward the problem. You know you are on the right track when people tell you you are on the wrong track.

That goes too far, of course. Is everything that disagrees with the dominant aproach therefore right? No. But a serious scholar ought routinely to inspect competing ways of talking about the same subject matter. The feeling that you can't say what you mean in the language you are using will warn you that the literature is crowding you. It may take a long time to find out that this has happened to you, if you find out at all. I only saw my mistake about the marijuana study fifteen years later (see the discussion in Becker 1967 and 1974). Use the literature, don't let it use you.

Nine

Friction and Word Processors

I wonder why people are so reluctant to rewrite. It seems obvious that, although you can't get it right the first time, you can easily fix it later. I have already discussed some of the reasons for that reluctance. But my own experience writing on a computer (and what others have told me of theirs) showed me that sheer physical friction is another powerful cause of that reluctance. That led to some thoughts, perhaps less based on facts of social organization than earlier chapters, about the implications of writing being physical labor.

I wrote the paper with which this book opens on a microcomputer. Though this first experience with one frightened me a little at first, writing soon seemed so much less work that I wondered how I had managed before. I'm not the only one. Word processors make writing easier for almost everyone, both people who have trouble writing and those who wrote easily before they got one (see Lyman 1984 for an account based on systematic observation). People who hide their early drafts for fear others will laugh at them clearly profit by the easy erasabiity of what they write. But why should writers who don't worry about being laughed at find computerized writing easier? For me, it is a matter of physical friction.

We think of writing as mental activity, as conceptual, dealing with ideas and emotions. That accepts the traditional distinction between work of the mind and work of the body, between head and hand. People who work with their heads get paid more, wear cleaner clothes, and live in better neighborhoods. In other words, working with your mind is higher class than working with your hands and body. We may not believe that ourselves, but like other items of culture, it is something "everyone knows" and on which, therefore, the society runs. We can't help but know that everyone thinks that. Irving Louis Horowitz has summarized the conventional head-hand theme this way:

> There are types of people just as there are differences in nature. Some are born to rule, others to be ruled. While in theory one may rise from ruled to ruling, operationally this is impossible. Those who work with their minds are more important than those who work with their physical power. In assessing the importance of people, one must distinguish those who can from those who cannot conceptualize—those who can from those who cannot dialecticize. The basis for the Platonic Academy is not simply condemnation of democracy, it is also the creation of a new ruling class based on a concept of inherited wisdom, and this concept is as commonplace now as it was 2,000 years ago. (Horowitz 1975, 398–99).

Horowitz remarks further that "the struggle between head and hand is essentially a symbolic form to represent class struggle. It is essentially a division between major competing forces for scarce resources" (404).

Accepting the head-hand distinction leads us to ignore the physicality of writing. But being a mental activity doesn't mean that writing is only mental. Like every other activity, it has a physical side, and that side affects the thinking part more than we usually admit. Some people, for instance, write in spurts. I sometimes do, sitting at the keyboard for eight or ten hours at a time, turning out several thousand words in a marathon session interrupted only by meals, coffee, the telephone, and the bathroom. Doing that teaches you quickly how physical writing is. You know it in your sore back and arms, in the crick in your neck the next day.

Conventional thinking about writing distinguishes the thinking part, which brings prestige to the person who does it, from the physical part, which doesn't. We distinguish these in common speech by talking about "writing" when we mean the prestigeful mental part and "typing" when we mean the physical act. Writing *can* be done separately from typing. Writers often write in their heads; you can't type in your head. Conversely, typists can type without noticing the content of what they are typing. Joy Charlton (1983) describes a typist who could converse lucidly on a topic completely divorced from that of the material she simultaneously typed. Typing, to paraphrase Wittgenstein, is what is left of writing if you take from it the thinking that most of us do as we compose at the typewriter. People who write for a living, however, usually type and write at the same time, but they emphasize the prestigeful part of what they are doing by calling it writing. I used to annoy academic friends by describing what I did when I wrote as "typing." ("Are you writing?" "Yes, I typed six pages today.") I deliberately used a low term to describe something prestigeful. The same common distinction allowed Truman Capote to insult many of his fellow writers by dismissing them as "typists."

For further evidence of the physical nature of writing, think of the addiction to particular writing tools that I've already discussed. People who use a pencil or felt-tip pen or typewriter get addicted to the feel of the implement. They are incapacitated when they have to use an instrument with a different touch.

Think, further, of the role typing plays in people's writing habits. No matter how you prepare your beginning drafts, they eventually must be typed, by you or someone else, and usually more than once. The final version meant for serious readers requires a clean copy, and people who rewrite a lot also need intermediate retypings. Retyping your own manuscripts is a tiring and boring chore (even though most people take advantage of the necessity to edit further). If you shift the physical work to someone else, you have to wait until they get around to it and then correct their errors and misunderstandings. But you need the retyping, and for still another physical reason.

Most writers try, usually unsuccessfully, to be neat. You can see what you are doing on a clean, neatly typed page. The sentences read consecutively and you can easily imagine what a reader will make of them. The physically orderly page magically makes you feel that your thoughts, too, are orderly and that your physical neatness made them that way. As it grows, the pile of neatly aligned pages looks more and more like a finished book or paper.

Rewriting destroys your neatness. You cross things out, leaving a line of meaningless Xs or an angry pencil slash in place of the crisp, cleanly expressed thought you had aimed for. You find that a thought that doesn't belong where you put it fits better somewhere else. So you cut it out, leaving a big hole or an awkward fragment. Holes and fragments don't stack well, so you tape what you cut out into its new home and repair the fragment so that the remnants will rest neatly on your pile of manuscript. Your manuscript is soon full of Xs, holes, and layers of paper bandaged over each other.

Eventually the mess bothers you enough that you type the page, or even the whole damn thing, over again. What began so neatly is now so marked up and confusing that its own author can't make sense of the scribblings and arrows. That confusion, in turn, destroys the precarious sense of logic and aesthetic order you are trying to preserve. (See the similar description in Zinsser 1983, 98.)

Most writers make retyping part of the ritual routine that sustains their work. If you rewrite as much as I do, a newly typed manuscript invites further revisions. It is easier to see what you are saying, and how you could change it, on the clean page. The old, heavily marked page, with its traces of other thoughts and other ways of expressing them, confuses you. So you make another construction on top of the new manuscript. That eventually requires still another retyping. Many writers keep that up for a long time.

Retyping is physically hard, not as hard as shoveling snow or hanging up laundry, but hard enough to create some friction, some inertia. Every writer has found a sentence that needed rewriting and, finding no place left on the page to put the new version, just let it pass. Cutting-and-pasting is even more demanding. Writers sometimes skip rewriting, then, because thinking about the physical and mental work it will take wearies them.

Writing on a computer removes that inertia. To understand how, we need a nonfrightening, layperson's introduction to these machines. A microcomputer or word processor is not just a typewriter, although it has a typewriter keyboard and you type on it as you do on a typewriter. ("You spent $2000 for a typewriter?") A microcomputer differs from a typewriter, however, in important ways. It doesn't make a permanent record of what you type. Instead, it records your text temporarily in its "memory" and also shows you part of what it has recorded on a screen. It will show you any part of its memory on the screen, once you learn to tell it to.

Because the computer doesn't permanently record what you write, you feel less committed when you type on it. Pressing a few keys wipes your ill-expressed thought off the screen and out of the memory as though it had never existed. No one will ever know the dumb thing you just wrote, or how crudely you expressed it. No crumpled wad of paper lies at the bottom of your wastebasket for your snoopy friends to see, maybe even pick out and look at. Since not everyone has fears like that—I don't, but some of my friends do—solving those problems is not the computer's greatest contribution.

The computer really excels at overcoming the physical friction of writing. Rewriting no longer means crossing out a phrase or sentence and writing in the new one. Instead you "delete" the phrase you don't like and "insert" its replacement. When you want to move a paragraph around, you don't cut it out and paste it on a new sheet of paper. You "move" it to the "get buffer," deleting it from its old position, and then "write" it in its new home. ("Get buffer" is what the program I use calls it—other programs use different names, including "cut-and-paste," for the same operation.) If you don't like the way the paragraph looks where you have put it, put it back where it was. If you decide to change a word or phrase, you use the "global find-and-replace" feature most word processing programs have to do it quickly and without missing any instances. (A friend of mine looked pretty skeptical about my enthusiasm until I mentioned "find-and-replace." He had changed the name of a character in his novel, which was published with a number of unexplained John's he had failed to find and change to Jim's.)

One feature of some word-processing programs that I appreciate a lot is the "word count." Give the command and find out just how many words you have written. I am not the only writer who likes to reward himself frequently by estimating (or actually counting) how many words I have already written. (1,864 to this point in the chapter, if you're curious.) Some writers set themselves a daily quota. This feature tells when you have made it, without the physical tedium of counting pages or lines and multiplying by your average.

All that is what every computer proselytizer will tell you, and every new owner is out to convert you. Why else am I writing this chapter?

We proselytizers make wordprocessing sound idyllic. It's not. Computers generate friction of their own. The worst thing (the first fear nonusers bring up) is to "lose" something you have written. That happens whenever a big university "mainframe" computer "goes down," losing everything in its working memory. You yourself might lose work you have just done, because you didn't understand the commands the machine obeys well enough and gave it an order that made it erase the "file" you were working on. Writers get quite attached to the smallest fragments of their prose, convincing themselves that they will never be able to recapture that perfect way of putting it, and regard these losses as unbelievable tragedies. They probably feel that way because they know how precarious their hold on these fugitive thoughts is. So the losses are real, and having to worry about them happening is a large price to pay for the ease of word processing.

The people who write word-processing programs—the instructions which make the computer do all these wonderful things—seldom write any other kind of prose themselves. If they did they would be writers, not programmers. So the instructions that tell you how to use a program, written in the language of the programming, rather than the writing, trade, are often difficult for nonusers to follow. The computer says such things to you as "ILLEGAL COMMAND" or "ERROR—SLOT AND DRIVE OUT OF RANGE." Until you get used to being talked to that way, you may not like it.

Worse yet, and more pertinent to our theme, some things we want to do are no easier to do on a word processor than they were with scissors and tape, and maybe even harder. Computers store what we type on them in "files" on "disks," and it takes a little doing to move material from one file to another because we have discovered a place where it fits better, or to save material when the computer tells you your disk is full.

By writing on a computer, you can quickly produce many versions of the same passage. If they were on paper, you would probably forget them in a manila folder until, some desperate day, you thought that one of them might be the magic right version. You would recognize the one you wanted by its look. You won't be able to inspect all the versions of a passage you save on a computer that easily. All you will be able to see is a list of file names, and shortly after you have invented them, they won't mean much to you. The Apple I wrote this book on is forgiving and lets you give files names that are thirty characters long, enough to make the title a little descriptive. The eight characters many other computers limit file names to make it much more difficult to know what a file contains. So you may pay for your new computer-assisted writing by not being able to tell documents apart, wallowing in a confusing stack of superficially identical versions of the same thing.

And you have to learn all the words I put in quotes above, and all the commands I referred to so casually. Many potential users describe what they hope the computer will do for them by saying, "All you have to is push a button, and it will. . . ." Oh no it won't! You need time to study and master that vocabulary, and the ideas and way of looking at the world that lie behind its terms. Who could blame you for not wanting to put all that time in? I wouldn't have done it myself if I had had anything better to do. But I had just finished a long book and so had a little time on my hands; the devil found work for them.

No proselytizer told me the most important benefit of writing on a computer: how much easier it would be to think by writing (in the way described by the cognitive psychologists interested in writing cited in earlier chapters). I habitually, as I've said, write an almost deliberately disorganized first draft—whatever comes into my head—hoping to discover the main themes I want to work on by seeing what comes out in that uncensored flow. I used to continue by writing a second draft which put those themes together in some more-or-less logical order. Then—third draft—I cut words, combined sentences, rephrased ideas, and in the course of that got an even clearer idea of what I meant to say. That's what made my pages so messy and provoked so much cutting-and-pasting. It took months of that to reach a final draft.

It takes less time now. As I write, I begin to see the structure my prose is moving toward. "Oh, that's what I want to say!" Instead of filing the thought for future use, I immediately go back to an appropriate place and start inserting that structure into what I am writing. No cutting, no pasting. It's much easier, and so I take the trouble to do it. Doing it, I don't interrupt the flow of my thinking to do physical chores. By the time I print out my first "hard copy," I have what, before the computer, would have been a third or fourth draft.

The change in my habits illustrates something people who write about computers systematically lie about. Lie may be too strong a word, and mystify also makes the misrepresentation sound more intentional than it probably is. But the misrepresentation does make it hard to learn what working with a computer will really be like. It hides what is essential, that to get the good of your computer you will have to change your way of thinking very substantially and become more of a computernik than you dreamed of becoming, or wanted to become.

All the "How to Buy a Computer" articles give the same advice. Decide what you want to do with your computer: write letters or books, keep your accounts, do budget forecasts, play games. . . . Then shop for software. See which programs do exactly what you want them to do. Then buy the computer those programs run on.

That advice sounds sensible. But you can't follow it, for reasons inherent in computers and our motives for using them. The advice assumes that you already know just what you want to do. You want to write your thesis or balance your checkbook. But remember, you already do those things, using satisfyingly effective precomputer routines. The advice in the magazine tells you that you can find a program that will let you do exactly what you are already doing.

That's a lie because you can't do things just the same way. If you're used to writing your scholarly articles on yellow ruled pads with a green felt tip pen, too bad. You can't do that on a computer. If you like to do your school papers by writing little snippets and scotchtaping them together, you can't do that either. If you write with a computer, you will have to learn to do what those ways of working did for you in a new way.

But the way the computer offers you is not a way you're used to. Of course, you're buying the computer because you want to write (or keep your checkbook) in a new and more advantageous way. But that means giving up the old ways. Some people resist that. They ask suspiciously whether they can rewrite but still save the old version in case they like it better, or whether they can still keep folders full of little bits of paper with notes on them, or any of the other rituals they have become attached to. But why trouble yourself with all the commands and new language and dangers of losing what you have written if you are just going to do what you always did? You don't get the good of the computer that way.

So you want to do something new, and the columns lie a second time by telling you that you need only find the program that does that new thing. But you can't follow that advice because you can't possibly know what you want to do until you have learned a new way of working and started thinking like the computer.

When you do, you won't want to write the way you used to. You will want to do what you didn't know could be done. You will work and think in ways that are foreign and feel funny at first. They eventually become second nature. William Zinsser's rhapsody on learning to use his computer's Delete key—learning to first delete letters, then words, and then to use the "Find" function to delete everything up to the first occurrence of a mark—exactly describes the phenomenon (Zinsser 1983, 71–75).

Different people take advantage of the computer's possibilities differently. For me, it's meant learning to think modularly, learning to deal more than I ever did with small units of material I can put together and take apart in several ways to see how the result looks. Similarly, I edit extensively on the screen, skipping the stage of printing out a version and working on the paper copy that many people hang on to. That allows me to look at five different ways of saying the same thing before I decide on one. I may even line them up one under the other to compare them.

Being able to do all these things may not be helpful. A third lie is that the computer will save you time. It won't, because you learn to think the way the computer does. You might save time *if* you did nothing with the computer but the one job you had in mind when you got it. You can certainly type your letters faster and make fewer errors *if* all you do is type letters. But then you don't get much good out of your computer. It is not worth the time or money just to type error-free letters a little faster. That's how you start thinking. You want to do more, and some things suggest themselves immediately. But doing those other things takes up all the time you saved on the original task, and then some.

When I first got interested in computers, my daughter, who had studied computing in school, warned me that I would probably go ape. Why? Because I like to do puzzles and the computer is an endless source of puzzles. You can always imagine trying something for which no way is immediately available but which seems like a thing a computer could do. Schiacchi (1981) describes a laboratory filled with hardheaded physical scientists who spent months trying to make their mainframe computer's word-processing program do a better job of formatting reports than it was doing. This had nothing to do with the content of the reports, only with the way they were displayed on the typed page. They wanted to make the computer do what any competent typist could have done sound asleep. Not being computer experts, they took quite a while to solve the problem and explained that they had to do it because they needed "professionally formatted" reports.

My own analogous foolishness is even crazier. It arose out of the proliferation of hardware and software compatible with the Apple computer I used. Because so many manufacturers produce printers and printer-interface cards compatible with the Apple, and word-processing programs that run on the Apple, no instruction manual ever contains instructions to do what you want to do for all the combinations of equipment on which you might want to do it. (Zinsser spared himself these temptations by sticking to IBM.) In addition, Apples are deservedly well-known for their ability to create graphic images. That means they can create a variety of type faces, beyond the normal ones built into every printer, thus multiplying the complications. I had some programs that produced such type faces on the screen. Now I wanted to print out what I wrote with my word-processing program in those type faces. If I worked in classics or biblical studies, there might have been some point to my intense desire to print what I wrote in Greek and Hebrew. Since I knew no Greek at all and no Hebrew beyond what had been required for my sketchy studies for the bar mitzva, this was just plain puzzle-solving. After futilely pestering the people who sold the word processor, I finally found an ad for a program that would print my texts in any type face I wanted. After a little experimentation and learning how to use several computer functions I hadn't needed before, I got it working and was very pleased. I wrote all my friends letters containing ten different type faces. I suppose that I spent at least fifteen or twenty hours solving this problem. Once I learned how to do it, however, it seemed less interesting to do. I decided that what I really wanted to do was print, right in the middle of my text, little pictures I could make with a graphics program. (My new Macintosh has made that easy enough; now I have to find a reason to do it.) My writing takes less time, but the time saved has gone into satisfying new desires.

Once I started thinking like a computer, I found other new things to learn and do that were less frivolous. Sociological writers keep data around in various forms: notes on reading, field notes, summaries of results, ideas about how to organize materials, bibliography, memos on this and that. Every scholar needs a system for organizing all this paper, and computer programs called "file managers" or "data bases" do something like that. Unfortunately, the biggest users of data bases are businesses, which use them to keep track of customers, inventory, orders, and expenses. Scholars need, instead, something more flexible, something not designed to manage vast amounts of highly similar material, not so tailored to financial concerns, concerned less with sorting mailing lists by zipcode than arranging tentative ideas. Such programs exist, but you have to dig them out of the mass of competing material and see how you can use them to do what you want. I have done that for myself and am happy with the result, but I can see that developing such a system is something scholars will want do for themselves, at a considerable cost in time and in the effort of consciously thinking through alternatives to old habits. (Becker, Gordon, and LeBailly 1984 discuss the criteria for computer systems to handle field notes and similar materials.)

So a microcomputer will probably make you feel that your work is easier, but it won't be the same work anymore and you may not save a minute. And I haven't even mentioned computer games!

Ten

A Final Word

Reading this book will not solve all your writing problems. It will hardly solve any of them. No book, no author, no expert—no one else can solve your problems. They are yours. You have to get rid of them.

But you might get some ideas about how to solve them, or at least start working on them, from things I've said. You can, for instance, avoid the curse of trying to get it right the first time, and thus not doing it at all, by writing anything that comes into your head for a first draft. You know, if you followed my arguments, that you can clean it up later and, therefore, that you needn't worry about the first draft's flaws.

You can avoid the wooliness and pretentiousness of "classy" writing by going over your prose repeatedly, taking out words that aren't working. You can think about what kind of person you want to be in your writing and how the persona you adopt will affect the credibility of what you say. You can take your meta-

phors seriously and see if they still make sense. By
simply *paying attention*, you can get a lot of what you
do under control.

I could keep on, in this fashion, summarizing what
I've already said. But you can pick out these tips as
easily as I can. Knowing the tips won't, as I said, solve
the problems. None of this will work unless you make
it your habitual practice. To get the good of these or any
other tips, use them, try them out in a variety of
circumstances on a variety of writing chores. Adapt
them to your preferences, style, subject matter, and
audience. You have read them, but they're still mine.
Until you make them yours by using them, they are
just ways of evading the hard work of changing your
ways.

The preceding suggests that will power and hard
work will take care of matters. Although I've tried to
avoid it, that Ben Franklin moral has lurked in everything I said. It's partly sound: nothing will happen
without the work. It's misleading if it leads you to think
that working hard is all it takes. Many sociologists work
very hard but accomplish little. You must also take
some chances, let others see your work, open yourself
to criticism. That may be frightening, even painful, in
the short run. But the long-range consequences of not
getting your work done are much more painful.

You needn't begin by writing a book. Writing anything—letters, journal entries, memoranda—will take
some of the mystery and danger out of writing. I write
a lot of letters. I also write memos, to myself and to
people I work with or share some interest with. I look
through these random, barely censored documents for
ideas, half-stated but possibly interesting, and for the
beginnings of something more serious.

A second lesson of this book, implicit in every
chapter and explicit in most of them, is that writing is
an organizational act, done in response to whatever
constraints, opportunities, and incentives the organization you write in presents to you. So another reason

these tips might not improve your writing is that the social organization you work in demands bad writing. Sociologists and other scholars often insist to me that they could not get their work accepted by professors, editors, and publishers if it were written in the plain style I've advocated. (See Hummel and Foster's letter to the editor about chapter 1, quoted earlier.) I don't believe that that is generally true, but it certainly might be true at times and in some organizations. Orwell believed that the pressure to disguise political realities led officials and their supporters to write in a way that disguised rather than communicated. Some people think scholars operate under similar constraints, perhaps not political, just built into the working assumptions of disciplines. A friend who is a psychologist once told me of being congratulated on a somewhat unconventional paper by the editor of a major journal, who immediately added, "For God's sake, don't send it to me. I wouldn't dare to print it, because it's not in the right form!"

If social organization causes problems, it also contains the materials for solutions. Scholars shouldn't assume, for instance, that they must do things in an inferior way without making some tests. The discipline may contain the organizational resources you need to do things differently. You can find out if you really have to write badly by trying something else and seeing what happens.

Social organization may, in still another way, keep you from making these (typically) simple and safe experiments. The patterned activities of scholarly life often hide the social supports that allow you to take chances. Indeed, as Pamela Richards made clear in describing the risks of writing, scholars often actively undermine each other. You can't take any of the chances I suggest, modest as they are, if you have good reason to fear your colleagues, junior and senior. You can avoid that by actively building networks of mutual help. As Richards also says, if you try you can find those helpful people, you can take risks and check out your fears, discarding those that can be overcome.

Some people have thought my suggestions for seemingly endless rewriting unrealistic or needlessly heroic. No one has that much time, they say. How can you stand to work so hard? That shows a great misunderstanding. No one has done the careful studies that would prove it, but I am convinced that scholars who write this way take less time to do seven or eight drafts than other people spend on one. They have no special gift. It's simply the difference between trying to get it right in your head the first time and doing it on paper or a computer monitor and fixing up little things as you go along. Nor are such writers unusually able to bear anxiety. Instead of bearing it, they avoid it by first doing only what is easy to do and moving in small steps from that to something marginally harder. The easier cleaning-up steps reduce the punch of the real anxiety producers.

Finally, apply sociology's great liberating message to your own scholarly situation. Understand that the troubles you may have are not entirely your own doing, not the result of some terrible personal defect, but something built into the organizations of academic life. Then you will not add to the trouble by blaming yourself for what you haven't done.

So the moral, Pollyannaish as it sounds, is Try It! As a friend once said to me, the worst that can happen is that people will think you're a jerk. It could be worse.

References

Antin, David. 1976. *talking at the boundaries*. New York: New Directions.

Arendt, Hannah. 1969. Introduction. Walter Benjamin: 1892–1940. Pp. 1–59 in Walter Benjamin, *Illuminations*. New York: Schocken Books.

Bazerman, Charles. 1981. What Written Knowledge Does: Three Examples of Academic Discourse. *Philosophy of the Social Sciences* 11, (no. 3): 361–387.

Becker, Howard S. *Outsiders: Studies in the Sociology of Deviance*. Glencoe: Free Press.

———. 1967. History, Culture and Subjective Experience: An Exploration of the Social Bases of Drug-Induced Experiences. *Journal of Health and Social Behavior* 8 (September): 163–76.

———. 1974. Consciousness, Power and Drug Effects. *Journal of Psychedelic Drugs* 6 (January–March): 67–76.

————. 1980 [1951]. *Role and Career Problems of the Chicago School Teacher*. New York: Arno Press.

————. 1982a. *Art Worlds*. Berkeley: University of California Press.

————. 1982b. Inside State Street: Photographs of Building Interiors by Kathleen Collins. *Chicago History* 11 (Summer): 89–103.

———— and James Carper. 1956a. The Elements of Identification with an Occupation. *American Sociological Review* 21 (June): 341–48.

————. 1956b. The Development of Identification with an Occupation. *American Journal of Sociology* 61 (January): 289–98.

————, Blanche Geer and Everett C. Hughes. 1968. *Making the Grade: The Academic Side of College Life*. New York: John Wiley and Sons, Inc.

————, Blanche Geer, Everett C. Hughes, and Anselm L. Strauss. 1961. *Boys in White: Student Culture in Medical School*. Chicago: University of Chicago Press.

————, Andrew C. Gordon, and Robert K. LeBailly. 1984. Fieldwork with the Computer: Criteria for Assessing Systems. *Qualitative Sociology* 7 (Spring and Summer): 16–33.

Berger, Bennett. 1981. *The Survival of a Counterculture: Ideological Work and Everyday Life among Rural Communards*. Berkeley: University of California Press.

Bernstein, Theodore. 1965. *The Careful Writer: A Modern Guide to English Usage*. New York: Atheneum.

Booth, Wayne. 1979. *Critical Understanding: The Powers and Limits of Pluralism*. Chicago: University of Chicago Press.

Britton, James, et. al. 1975. *The Development of Writing Ability*. London: MacMillan.

Buckley, Walter. 1966. "Appendix: A Methodological Note." In Thomas Scheff, *Being Mentally Ill*, pp. 201–5. Chicago: Aldine Publishing Co.

Bulmer, Martin. 1984. *The Chicago School of Sociology: Institutionalization, Diversity, and the Rise of*

Sociological Research. Chicago: University of Chicago Press.

Campbell, Paul Newell. 1975. The *Personae* of Scientific Discourse. *Quarterly Journal of Speech* 61 (December): 391–405.

Carey, James T. 1975. *Sociology and Public Affairs: The Chicago School.* Beverly Hills: Sage Publications.

Charlton, Joy. 1983. "Secretaries and Bosses: The Social Organization of Office Work." Ph. D. dissertation, Northwestern University.

Clifford, James. 1983. On Anthropological Authority. *Representations* 1 (Spring): 118–46.

Cowley, Malcolm. 1956. Sociological Habit Patterns in Transmogrification. *The Reporter* 20 (September 20): 41 ff.

Davis, Murray S. 1971. That's Interesting! Towards a Phenomenology of Sociology and a Sociology of Phenomenology. *Philosophy of the Social Sciences* 1: 309–44.

Elbow, Peter. 1981. *Writing with Power: Techniques for Mastering the Writing Process.* New York: Oxford University Press.

Faris, Robert E. L. 1967. *Chicago Sociology: 1920–1932.* San Francisco: Chandler.

Fischer, David Hackett. 1970. *Historians' Fallacies.* New York: Harper and Row.

Flower, Linda. 1979. Writer–Based Prose: A Cognitive Basis for Problems in Writing. *College English* 41 (September): 19–37.

———— and John R. Hayes. 1981. A Cognitive Process Theory of Writing. *College Composition and Communication* 32 (December): 365–87.

Follet, Wilson. 1966. *Modern American Usage: A Guide.* Edited by Jacques Barzun. New York: Hill and Wang.

Fowler, H. W. 1965. *A Dictionary of Modern English,* 2nd ed. Edited by Ernest Gowers. New York: Oxford University Press.

Garfinkel, Harold. 1967. *Studies in Ethnomethodology.* Englewood Cliffs, N.J.: Prentice–Hall.

Geertz, Clifford. 1983. Slide Show: Evans–Pritchard's African Transparencies. *Raritan* 3 (Fall): 62–80.

Gerth, H. H. and C. Wright Mills, editors. 1946. *From Max Weber: Essays in Sociology*. New York: Oxford University Press.

Goffman, Erving. 1952. On Cooling the Mark Out: Some Aspects of Adaptation to Failure. *Psychiatry* 15 (November): 451–63.

Gowers, Sir Ernest. 1954. *The Complete Plain Words*. Baltimore: Penguin Books.

Gusfield, Joseph. 1981. *The Culture of Public Problems: Drinking–Driving and the Symbolic Order*. Chicago: University of Chicago Press.

Hammond, Philip, editor. 1964. *Sociologists at Work*. New York: Basic Books.

Horowitz, Irving Louis. 1969. *Sociological Self–Images: A Collective Portrait*. Beverly Hills: Sage Publications.

———. 1975. Head and Hand in Education: Vocationalism versus Professionalism. *School Review* 83 (May): 397–414.

Hughes, Everett C. 1971. Dilemmas and Contradictions of Status. In *The Sociological Eye: Selected Papers*, pp. 141–50. Chicago: Aldine Publishing Co.

Hummel, Richard C., and Gary S. Foster. 1984. Reflections on Freshman English and Becker's Memoirs. *Sociological Quarterly* 25 (Summer): 429–31.

Kidder, Tracy. 1981. *The Soul of a New Machine*. Boston: Little, Brown and Company.

Kuhn, Thomas. 1962 (2nd ed., 1970). *The Structure of Scientific Revolutions*. Chicago: University of Chicago Press.

Lakoff, George, and Mark Johnson. 1980. *Metaphors We Live By*. Chicago: University of Chicago Press.

Latour, Bruno. 1983. Give Me a Laboratory and I Will Raise the World. In Karin D. Knorr–Cetina and Michael Mulkay, *Science Observed: Perspectives on the Social Study of Science*, 141–70. Beverly Hills: Sage Publications.

———. 1984. *Les microbes: guerre et paix*. Paris: A. M. Métailié.

——— and Françoise Bastide. 1983. Essai de science–fabrication: mise en evidence experimentale du processus de construction de la réalité par l'application de methodes socio–semiotiques aux textes scientifiques. *Etudes Francaises* 19 (Fall): 111–33.

——— and Steve Woolgar. 1979. *Laboratory Life: The Social Construction of Scientific Facts*. Beverly Hills: Sage Publications.

Lyman, Peter. 1984. Reading, Writing, and Word Processing: Toward a Phenomenology of the Computer Age. *Qualitative Sociology* 7 (Spring and Summer): 75–89.

McCloskey, Donald N. 1983. The Rhetoric of Economics. *Journal of Economic Literature* 21 (June): 481–517.

———. N. d. The Problem of Audience in Historical Economics: Rhetorical Thoughts on a Text by Robert Fogel. Unpublished paper.

Malinowski, Bronislaw. 1948. *Magic, Science and Religion and Other Essays*. Garden City, N.Y.: Doubleday & Company.

Merton, Robert. K. 1969. Foreword to a Preface for an Introduction to a Prolegomenon to a Discourse on a Certain Subject. *The American Sociologist* 4 (May): 99.

———. 1972. Sociology, Jargon, and Slanglish. In R. Serge Denisoff, ed., *Sociology: Theories in Conflict*, pp. 52–8. Belmont, Ca.: Wadsworth Publishing Co.

Mills, C. Wright. 1940. Situated Actions and Vocabularies of Motive. *American Sociological Review* 5: 904–13.

———. 1959. *The Sociological Imagination*. New York: Oxford University Press.

Moulin, Raymonde. 1967. *Le marché de la peinture en france*. Paris: Les Editions de Minuit.

Nystrand, Martin. 1982. *What Writers Know: The Lan-*

guage, Process, and Structure of Written Discourse. New York: Academic Press.

Orwell, George. 1954. Politics and the English Language. In his A Collection of Essays, 162–77. Garden City, N.Y.: Doubleday & Company.

Overington, Michael A. 1977. The Scientific Community as Audience: Towards a Rhetorical Analysis of Science. Philosophy and Rhetoric 10 (Summer): 143–164.

Perl, Sondra. 1980. Understanding Composing. College Composition and Communication 31 (December): 363–69.

Perlis, Vivian. 1974. Charles Ives Remembered: An Oral History. New Haven: Yale University Press.

Polya, George. 1954. Mathematics and Plausible Reasoning, vol. 2, Patterns of Plausible Inference. Princeton: Princeton: Princeton University Press.

Rains, Prudence Mors. 1971. Becoming an Unwed Mother. Chicago: Aldine Publishing Company.

Rose, Mike. 1983. Rigid Rules, Inflexible Plans, and the Stifling of Language: A Cognivitist Analysis of Writer's Block. College Composition and Communication 34 (December): 389–401.

Rosenthal, Robert. 1966. Experimenter Effects in Behavioral Research. New York: Appleton–Century–Crofts.

Schiacchi, Walter. 1981. The Process of Innovation: A Study in the Social Dynamics of Computing. Ph. D. dissertation, University of California-Irvine.

Schultz, John. 1982. Writing from Start to Finish. Upper Montclair, NJ: Boynton/Cook Publishers.

Selvin, Hanan C., and Everett K.Wilson. 1984. On Sharpening Sociologists' Prose. The Sociological Quarterly 25 (Spring): 205–22.

Shaughnessy, Mina P. 1977. Errors and Expectations: A Guide for the Teacher of Basic Writing. New York: Oxford University Press.

Shaw, Harry. 1975. Dictionary of Problem Words and Expressions. New York: McGraw–Hill.

Simmel, Georg. 1950. *The Sociology of Georg Simmel.* Translated by Kurt Wolff. Glencoe: The Free Press.

Sternberg, David. 1981. *How to Complete and Survive a Doctoral Dissertation.* New York: St. Martin's Press.

Stinchcombe, Arthur L. 1978. *Theoretical Methods in Social History.* New York: Academic Press.

————. 1982. Should Sociologists Forget Their Fathers and Mothers? *The American Sociologist* 17 (February): 2–11.

Strunk, William Jr. and E. B. White. 1959. *The Elements of Style.* New York: Macmillan.

Stubbs, Michael. 1980. *Language and Literacy: The Sociolinguistics of Reading and Writing.* London: Routledge and Kegan Paul.

Sutherland, J. A. 1976. *Victorian Novelists and Publishers.* Chicago: University of Chicago Press.

Waller, Willard. 1932. *Sociology of Teaching.* New York: John Wiley and Sons.

Weber, Max. 1946. *From Max Weber: Essays in Sociology.* Translated and edited by H. H. Gerth and C. Wright Mills. New York: Oxford University Press.

Whyte, William Foote. 1943. *Street Corner Society.* Chicago: University of Chicago Press.

Williams, Joseph M. 1981. *Style: Ten Lessons in Clarity and Grace.* Glenview: Scott, Foresman.

Zinsser, William. 1980. *On Writing Well: An Informal Guide to Writing Nonfiction.* New York: Harper and Row.

————. 1983. *Writing with a Word Processor.* New York: Harper and Row.

Index